new madrid

New Madrid: A Journal of Contemporary Literature
Volume VI, Number 1
Winter 2011

New Madrid (pronounced New Mad-drid) is the national journal of the low-residency MFA program at Murray State University. It takes its name from the New Madrid seismic zone, which falls within the central Mississippi Valley and extends through western Kentucky. Between 1811 and 1812, four earthquakes with magnitudes greater than 7.0 struck this region, changing the course of the Mississippi River, creating Reelfoot Lake in Tennessee and ringing church bells as far away as Boston.

The editors invite submissions of poetry, fiction and creative non-fiction. **Please note: We accept online submissions ONLY.** All submissions must be sent via Submission Manager, which can be accessed from our website. Submissions should be in MS Word format with a 12-point font, such as Times New Roman or Arial. The attachment should end with ".doc" in the file name. Submissions will be accepted only during two reading periods: Jan. 15 to March 15 and Aug. 15 to Oct. 15. Check our website for specific guidelines and announcements of special issues.

Website: *www.newmadridjournal.org*

Copyright © 2011 by Murray State University

ISBN: 978-0-9791319-1-2
ISSN: 1935-3936

Subscriptions: $15.00 annually for two issues.

Please send subscription requests to:

The Editors, *New Madrid*
Department of English and Philosophy
Murray State University
7C Faculty Hall
Murray, KY 42071-3341

Front Cover: Sant Khalsa, Photographs from the *Western Waters* series.

Back Cover: Sant Khalsa, A *Study for Sacred Spring*, photograph.

new madrid

EDITOR
Ann Neelon

FICTION EDITOR
Dale Ray Phillips

ADVISORY AND CONTRIBUTING EDITORS
Squire Babcock
Carrie Jerrell
Martin Roper

GRAPHIC DESIGN
Jim Bryant

MANAGING EDITOR
Jacque E. Day

MFA EDITORIAL BOARD
Jonathan Ashley
Jolene Barto
Nora Hall Burton
Carrie Gaffney
Shannon Hall
Barbara A. Lee
Christopher J. Lessick
Megan Scholl Lindberg
Gretchen M. Oberle
Chet Weise

TABLE OF CONTENTS

Book Reviews

Cover Art

EDITOR'S INTRODUCTION
Ann Neelon

In "Coming into the Watershed," a chapter in *A Place in Space*, Gary Snyder writes, "A watershed is a marvelous thing to consider: this process of rain falling, streams flowing, and oceans evaporating causes every molecule of water on earth to make the complete trip once every two million years. The surface is carved into watersheds—a kind of familial branching, a chart of relationship, and a definition of place." Kentucky, a poor state, is rich in water, and that richness defines us at least as much as our poverty rate.

In western Kentucky, we are blessed with a dense concentration of major rivers and reservoirs. Together, Kentucky Lake and Lake Barkley feature 3,700 miles of shoreline and 250,000 surface acres. Our Four Rivers Region watershed also encompasses the Lower Cumberland River Basin, the Lower Tennessee River Basin, and tributaries draining into the Ohio and Mississippi Rivers. It also includes 7,259 miles of streams.

Kentucky's legacy of fresh water in abundance is all the more impressive in that scientists estimate that something like 97 percent of the water on earth is salty and two percent constricted in the forms of snow and ice. As citizens of Kentucky, we are the trustees of a significant percentage of the one percent available to quench thirst, water crops, etc.

A pertinent question right now is, to what degree are we squandering this trust? According to a December 10, 2010, editorial in the Lexington *Herald-Leader*, the Beshear administration has acknowledged 2,765 violations of the Clean Water Act by 103 mines in a settlement recently announced. Although only four states exceed Kentucky in the number of water-pollution permits they must enforce under the Clean Water Act, forty eight exceed it in terms of funding for monitoring. The discrepancies among coal-producing states are telling. While Kentucky spends $193 to support enforcement for each permit, Virginia spends $2,800. Kentucky's Energy and Environment Cabinet admitted both to filing inaccurate water-monitoring reports in hundreds of cases and to allowing mining companies to go for up to three years without quarterly filing of the water-monitoring reports required by law.

Kentucky has also been cited as a major contributor to the hypoxia that has given rise to the Gulf of Mexico's oxygen-depleted "dead zone." According to James Bruggers of the Louisville *Courier-Journal*, new computer modeling has implicated inadequately treated sewage, lawn fertilizers and runoff contaminated by agricultural manure as the causes of the decomposing algal blooms that kill off much aquatic life. These same practices cause local problems in Kentucky with groundwater.

I can still remember how devastated my father, a huge football fan, was in 1969, when every player on the varsity football team at his alma mater, Holy Cross College in Worcester, Massachusetts, became infected with hepatitis from a water fountain on the practice field, dooming the season. Local kids, infected with hepatitis, had urinated into water that had spilled over and pooled at the base of the fountain. A reduction in water pressure due to firefighting efforts in a burning tenement two miles away was all it took to guarantee the suction of the contaminated water back into the fountain.

We are all radically interconnected when it comes to water. It should concern all of us, in a deep way, that roughly one billion people on the planet do not have access to clean drinking water, and 2.6 billion lack basic sanitation. Nor are industrialized nations immune to the effects of water scarcity. Wars already are, and will increasingly be, fought over water, and we will have to defend our national security in the face of these wars. Credit ratings on the municipal bonds that underwrite the U.S. water supply do not currently take water scarcity into account, and our economic well-being may be threatened when this risk is recognized.

When the football team at Sacramento State learned of Holy Cross' fate, they dedicated their 1969 season to the Crusaders. Thus football players at a public university in California with no official connection whatsoever to Holy Cross, a Jesuit college on the East Coast, wore Holy Cross' purple jerseys instead of their own for the last game of the season.

This is the kind of empathetic behavior we need to emulate when it comes to those on our planet without access to potable water. We need to acknowledge the superior advantage enjoyed by those in industrialized nations (Americans currently consume fifteen times as much water as those in the developing world) and work to lessen the burden of those who have no choice but to expend, collectively, more than two hundred million hours of labor each day gathering water. This lost productivity indicts us all.

Thirty years ago, my circumstances as a Peace Corps Volunteer in Senegal forced me to take up Henry David Thoreau's mantle and live deliberately when it came to water. Although I was one of the lucky few in West Africa with access to tapwater, I was forced to boil every ounce of it I drank. I was also cautioned to add iodine to the tapwater in which I was required to soak all fruits and vegetables for half an hour before eating. I lived all the more deliberately because I had witnessed a friend, who had taken a few forbidden swigs from a faucet in Dakar, the capital city, lose one third of her body weight in a three-month battle against cholera. As I contemplate the fresh slate of a new year—keeping in mind that over seventeen million barrels of oil are expended in the manufacture of bottled water, with 86 percent of the bottles never making it into recycling bins—I hope to commit to living more deliberately once again, especially when it comes to refilling water bottles from my own tap.

This issue commemorates the declaration by the General Assembly of the United Nations in July 2010 that access to safe and clean drinking water and sanitation is a basic human right. It also solemnizes the terrifying fury of the floods that have ravaged the planet this year in Kentucky and Tennessee, as well as in Pakistan, Poland, Portugal, Brazil, China, France, Romania, Ukraine, Hungary, Peru, Mexico, Canada, Columbia, Australia, Indonesia, Serbia, Argentina, Kenya, Nigeria, Spain, Guatemala, and Singapore. We've all gotten used to images of streets turned into rivers, people with no belongings any more being transported in boats instead of cars. Water, water everywhere, but not a drop for anguished refugees to drink.

Thanks to our MFA interns Jonathan Ashley, Jolene Barto, Nora Hall Burton, Carrie Gaffney, Shannon Hall, Barbara A. Lee, Christopher J. Lessick, Megan Scholl Lindberg, Gretchen M. Oberle, and Chet Weise for their acuity in evaluating submissions, their assiduousness in copy-editing and their all-around good cheer. Thanks, as ever, to Jacque Day for taking on every editorial challenge with exceptional grace and good humor.

Mistake
Mario Chard

What is beautiful about the Iranian boy
who dips his fingers in the river,
who is blind, who reads the stones there,
is that he translates what he finds
for no one. I may be wrong.
                                    It was,
after all, a film I hardly remember.
A boy reading Braille in the riverbed.
Once in a school meeting common
to the inner city, I was called to interpret
for a Mexican father.
                        The Board, raised
on a platform, sat before us sipping
water. They had closed his son's school.
I remember I barely knew the man's
Spanish, that he, finally, kept none of his
anger back, but also that
                            when he stopped
speaking—my turn to translate
his words—I was at first confused, simply
started back in Spanish with what he asked.
The father laughed. The Board followed.
The room of parents broke
                            into laughter.
I keep that sound like I keep the words
I offer no one, what little stones I find
weeding the garden, the word my young
son speaks who finds me there, points
to sweat on my forehead, says *water*.

Parable of My Father and Migrants

Mario Chard

Always from the bushes, burdened, four or six
unshaven, their shoes white with sawdust. Before
Aggie saw need to call I'd set to laying

chairs across the lawn. Never heard them speak. Not
to me. When they'd sit and Aggie brought and filled
for each a jug of water, I'd stay to sweep

the grass my boots tracked in the kitchen, kneel at
the window, watch the glasses shake at their lips
before the water fell in. And sometimes I

was angry at that, thought thirsty men shouldn't
waste their water or let it fall and rinse their
shoes like that. Then they'd leave. Once I asked Aggie

to let me leave the chairs outside, the jugs just
where the men left them—I'd take them in before
dark—and she agreed. But I forgot until

morning, woke to Aggie dragging chairs inside
her kitchen, the jugs still wet by my mistake,
raking in the cold, soaked grass I couldn't sweep.

Back West We Irrigate, Which Is to Say

Mario Chard

There is terror in a running faucet.
For that tone above all others, even

the licked drone of tires over highway
gravel, does not change—so does not

wake the irrigator should he leave
his water flooding overnight. We lived

on a mountain. Newlyweds. One house
in a row of equal houses. Our doors

locked at ten. What woke me, then,
those nights I let the faucet run? My wife's

turn in bed beside me. A low clap
of wings outside. Not these. Then,

like snow where snow hadn't been,
when the white cloud breaks to white

again, the mountain peak behind it, this
sound of running water left too long.

This sound even sex couldn't hide.
Lying there after it, we touch only by

accident. The body must re-learn its borders.
One sound hushed and then—the faucet,

running. I could say that it was other men
who left their wives in bed to turn

their backyard faucets off. Who ran out
naked, thinking the night dark enough

to hide them. But I wouldn't know
that some felt more than grass and soaked

chalk beneath their feet. That some
walked back slowly to their beds,

a network of irrigate pipes beneath them,
unseen. Their lawns clipped neatly

at the bleached foundations, their wives
somewhere behind that, already asleep.

That nothing had to wake us, really.
That only clothing, the need to

return, re-dress, to cover, could
pull me in from never going back.

In the Water
Teresa Milbrodt

DAD AND I have been performing at the Oklahoma State Fair for four days. I hold my breath and play solitaire under water. Dad built my rectangular tank out of salvaged clear glass shower doors soldered together. It's three doors long, two doors wide, needs two thousand three hundred gallons of water to fill it, and four guys to load it into the back of our pickup. The tank is big enough for me, a small table, and a chair. I wear a weight belt and use weighted cards.

We have a red canvas tent set up for the act. People pay admission and can stay as long as they like. Dad says it's a better deal that way, they can talk to me in-between games of solitaire and it's more likely they'll buy a shirt or video because I'm endearing. At least according to Dad. I'm also really bad at solitaire.

There are eight people in the audience, and one lady taps on the side of the tank, points to show me when I've missed a card. I smile to thank her. I've been doing this for five years and it gets boring. I'd rather have more audience interaction, play chess or checkers with them, but Dad wants something I can do in six minutes. Just long enough to lose a game of solitaire. It's one of the things we argue about. I'd rather be floating, meditating, and holding my breath. If I get really relaxed I can hold my breath for ten minutes, but me lying facedown in the tank looks scary. When I'm playing solitaire all the brain activity increases my metabolism and I can't hold my breath for as long, because I have to think about the damn cards.

This is what I'm doing when my aunt walks into the tent.

"Cheri!" I hear her through the water, look up from the cards, and lose my concentration. Damn. The audience members turn their wavery heads to glance at her, then turn back to me when they decide she's not very interesting. I knew my aunt lived around here. She's my dad's older sister, but I don't think he told her we were coming because he doesn't like her much. My aunt took care of my dad when they were little. She's six years older than him and their parents were sick a lot. Dad says she's controlling. Whenever he calls her, she tries to convince him to stop traveling.

I've only seen her a few times, and she didn't leave a good impression. We visited her when I was ten. She gave me lemonade with too little sugar in it and talked to me like I was five years old. I can't stand adults who talk down to kids.

My aunt holds out her arms and says something, probably wants me to come up and give her a hug. I shake my head, want to finish the stupid game because I haven't lost yet. Even though I get weary of solitaire, I'm committed to a game once I've started.

Dad ignores his sister for a minute, stands by my tank faithfully explaining the biology stuff, how the human body uses oxygen differently when someone holds her breath. Blood vessels in the arms and legs shrink and force oxygen from the limbs to the brain and heart. The longer one trains, the more blood she can move to the core of her body, and the slower her heart can beat. Dad has timed mine as low as twenty beats per minute.

He stops his lecture when my aunt grabs him in a hug. I hear the rise and fall of their voices but don't try to understand what they're saying. It takes another minute before I know I've lost the game. I surface, take off my weight belt, stand on the card table and exhale a long slow breath

My aunt reaches up to hug me. I hug back, get her wet.

"I saw you on television," my aunt says. "You should have told me you'd be in the area. I brought you a few books." She lugs a shopping bag next to the tank.

"Thanks." I cross my arms. People from the nightly news were here a couple days ago, doing some story about the sideshow as a lost art and me and dad carrying on a dying tradition.

"I want you both to come and stay with me for a week," she says.

"We have a hectic touring schedule this summer," says my father.

"But I never see either of you," says my aunt.

"How long did you say you could hold your breath?" says a boy about my age who's standing in the audience. He has hair the color of sand and snapping green eyes.

"Ten and a half minutes," I say because sometimes I exaggerate just a little.

"Damn," he says and nods.

I blush. I don't get much of a chance to talk with guys my age. When I bug Dad about this, he says guys my age just want One Thing.

"Wouldn't you like to visit?" says my aunt, smiling too brightly. "We'd have fun."

"We can talk later," I say, looking back at the guy my age. He's kind of cute. "Right now I'm performing."

I dunk under water, reattach the weight belt, and start another game of solitaire. My father and aunt talk in a corner, their voices flowing around me in the tank. I don't win my next two games and come up for air briefly between them. I can recover in two or three minutes after holding my breath for six, but I linger a bit to smile at the guy my age. He smiles back but leaves during my second game. Dammit. My dad and aunt are still talking.

After the third game, I surface.

"Aren't you staying down too long?" my aunt says.

I roll my eyes but am saved by two little girls, both about seven years old, asking the usual seven-year-old questions.

"Can you teach me to do that?"

"Do you ever have an accident and pee in the water? I peed in the pool once."

"Does it hurt when you open your eyes? I have goggles so it doesn't hurt when I do."

A mother drags them away.

I get back in the tank, fasten my belt, submerge. My aunt taps the glass and says something about my lungs and won't this be bad for them eventually.

When I surface again, my dad and aunt have completed their negotiations.

"I told your aunt she could meet us at our hotel this evening," Dad says.

"I guess," I sigh. "I'm going to be tired."

"I'll bring the books," says my aunt.

"Okay," I say and submerge again. I like it underwater – the smoothness of the cards in my hands, the textured glass shower stall doors, my wrinkled fingers, how sounds change and amplify, the way everything outside the tank seems a bit distended.

~ ~ ~

I started holding my breath when I was a little kid taking swimming lessons at the city pool. Other kids were always dunking me. At home I sat in a full bathtub for hours, going under again and again, making myself relax and stay down for an extra second. I got so good that when kids dunked me they had to drag me up again before their parents noticed and got pissed.

Dad was the one who figured out how to make my talent into a business and incorporate the playing cards. It wasn't anything he asked me about doing, which still makes me a little mad. Usually I like being on the road. We've been traveling for most of the last five years. I have to keep in shape, run three miles a day and lift weights in the motel if there is a weight room. With the right training anyone can hold their breath for three or four minutes, but Dad says I must have some sort of gift, a genetic kink, so I'm better at it than other people.

Dad is usually worried about genetic kinks. My grandpa died of a heart attack when he was forty-eight. My grandma was a diabetic and had a history of depression, was in and out of the hospital while my dad was growing up. That meant my dad was one worried little kid.

"When I was your age I always thought I was dying," he told me.

My dad doesn't trust his body. He's always taking his pulse or his blood sugar since he's a borderline diabetic. He became a high school biology teacher to understand more about anatomy and the cause of diseases, but that didn't relieve his fears. I think that's why he was so keen on teaching me how to control my body and its basic needs.

Around the time Dad was making a tank big enough to fit me and a small table, he and Mom divorced. Mom said she felt ignored. She was.

My aunt drove out to Ohio and tried to stop the separation.

"You need to think about this for a while longer," she said to my parents as they sat in the living room on opposite sides of the couch. "Think about how everything will affect Cheri."

But I knew my parents shouldn't be married. They fought too much, even in the cereal aisle of the grocery store when Dad wanted to get chocolate sugary stuff and Mom said he'd rot his teeth and mine. Dad was never the romantic type and made a better twelve-year-old than husband. He really liked kids, while Mom wasn't very maternal. Dad doesn't mind that she rarely pays child support. He just wants to keep traveling.

~ ~ ~

In the hotel I fill the bathtub to the brim with warm water and sit on the edge in my bathing suit until I hear the knock on the room door. I get in the tub.

"Your aunt's here," Dad says.

"Hi Cheri," my aunt calls.

I go under but can still hear my aunt's voice.

Dad opens the door. My aunt follows him in. I forgot the lock. Dammit. I surface.

"I'm practicing," I say.

"But you practiced all day," my aunt says.

"Practice makes perfect," I say and go under.

I give in when my father grabs my wrist, hauls me up.

"I don't want to interrupt you," says my aunt. "But it's been so long since we've had a good chat. You're a young woman now, and I'm curious about your plans for college."

"I'm kind of busy right now," I say, thinking of her sour lemonade and dumb questions.

"We'll be in town another four days," says my dad. "You could stop by the tent again."

My aunt bites her lip. "It's so crowded there," she says. "I wanted to chat here."

"It's been a long day," I say. "You should catch us in the morning."

My aunt sighs but nods. "I'll do that. We can arrange a longer visit for next week. Do enjoy the books, and I'll see you in the morning." She hugs me and gets a big wet spot on her t-shirt.

After she leaves and I dry off, I poke through the book bag. All high school textbooks.

Dad gets snacks for us from the vending machine, gummy worms and little chocolate chip cookies and a couple bags of potato chips. He watches television while I page through an American history book, then a chemistry book, then one on economics.

"Anything good?" he says.

"I think so," I say.

"Maybe we can go over that stuff next week," he says.

"Maybe," I say.

Dad tutors me on the road, does an okay job I guess, or at least as well as a biology teacher can when trying to instruct me in math and history and writing. Dad says I'm lucky because I'm getting the sort of education he wanted, seeing the world instead of being stuck in a classroom, but I would have liked to be on the swim team and go to football games and prom.

Whenever I mention this to Dad, suggest we stop traveling so I can go to high school for a year, he says I'll thank him for my unconventional education when I'm older.

The next morning Dad is not in a good mood, swears while he shaves and then again when he loses the top button off his shirt. I know it's because of my aunt's visit. He's worried she'll keep pestering us to stop traveling. Dad overreacts to stuff like this. My aunt will be easy enough to ignore, but even the thought of stopping makes Dad sore.

At the fairgrounds he tries to be really cheerful to compensate, but Dad gets fake happy before he gets withdrawn.

"That was a great breakfast at the motel," he says.

"It was nice," I say.

I'm worried about how he'll be later in the day. It's bad for the act when he doesn't feel like talking. No one wants to walk into the tent and see a moping middle-aged man, but sometimes he's like that while we're on the road. Quiet. Sad. I worry because my grandma had a history of depression. Dad says traveling is what makes him happy.

"I need to keep moving," he says.

I think he needs a distraction, something to keep him from sadness, which is part of the reason I don't press him to stop. There have only been a few times when he's gotten really bad, lain in bed for two or three days and not wanted to go to the fair and watch me perform. I have to take a cab and pay one of the people working in the concessions or at the rides to sit in the tent, make sure nothing goes wrong. I take dad in to a doctor and they adjust his medications and he's okay again for a while.

We don't see my aunt all day, which makes Dad happy. Maybe we're rid of her. I'm happy he's out of his funk and talking about business.

"We'll need to order more shirts soon," says Dad. "They're selling pretty well."

"Okay," I say. I hate the shirts. Dad designed them. They read *It's Better Underwater* and have a picture of me in my blue one-piece tank suit blowing bubbles, my solitaire cards laid out on the table in front of me.

"It's better underwater?" I said when Dad came up with the slogan. "Isn't that a little suggestive?" Dad won't let me wear two-piece suits that show three inches of my stomach.

"I thought it sounded kind of catchy," he said

I shrugged. It's not like I'm ever going to see the people who are wearing the shirts ever again, so I figure it's not worth caring about.

That night my aunt appears at the door to our motel room with Chinese takeout.

"Sorry I didn't come out in the morning," she says, "but I was busy and then it was too hot, so I figured it would be best to bring you dinner."

I'm almost happy to see her because I like Chinese food. Dad hates it so we don't order Chinese very often. He picks at the pork fried rice.

"So you really like traveling like this?" says my aunt.

"It's great," says Dad.

"I was asking Cheri," says my aunt.

"It's pretty good," I say. "Beats a geography book."

"See," says my dad, "we don't want to stop."

I grimace for a moment because sometimes I do want to stop. When I get tired of travel, I get whiny. Dad and I find a campground somewhere and take a week or two off. I meet other teenagers and we hang out, but we can't keep in touch because I don't have a real address to give them and know they wouldn't write.

The next day I wake up with a familiar pain in my hips. I've started my period early. I always have bad cramps and feel bloated and awful. Dad gets testy, too, since I can't perform as much, if at all. He doesn't like to think about my reproductive system.

My aunt arrives at the tent at nine-thirty, finds me dry and outside the tank.

She says, "You're not performing?" and looks honestly disappointed.

I tell her no, I'm having my period. Dad gave me some pills but they're not working yet.

"I might perform in the afternoon if I feel better," I say.

She asks if I want to go to her house for a little while to cool off.

"I don't know," I say. I'd rather not be alone with her so she can start in on a lecture.

"You'd be happier if you weren't in the humidity," she says.

I glance at my grumping father. I'd rather not be alone with him, either.

My aunt takes my hand and tugs gently. "Just get out of the heat for a little while," she says.

I feel too icky to protest.

My aunt guides me to her car and gives me a couple of painkillers from her purse before she starts the engine. After a few minutes my hips don't feel four feet wide. The pills Dad gives me never work this well. In her kitchen, my aunt arranges gingersnaps on a plate, pours two glasses of iced tea, and pushes the sugar bowl towards me. I eat a couple cookies and feel a lot more charitable towards her than I did before.

"So what do you want to study in college?" she says.

Dad's never mentioned the subject, but it's one I've considered. I tell her that I like science and social studies and geology, might want to be a teacher or researcher.

She smiles. "I was worried I'd have to convince you away from a life on the road."

I shrug and take another cookie.

"I'm worried about your education," she says more quietly. "I don't think your father is making you study as hard as you should. You might not be able to get into a good college, or any college at all. Do you even know the grade level you're studying at?"

I chew more slowly. I'm supposed to have just finished my sophomore year, but I don't know if I'm really there yet. My aunt is a high school English teacher, so she knows what she's talking about. Probably knows better than my dad.

"That's part of the reason I thought you might like to stay with me for a week or two," she says. "You could get a better idea of where you are in school, and where you need to be."

Maybe my aunt isn't the kind of person who can talk to a ten-year-old, but she knows I'm an adult. I can't say the same thing for my dad. He's the one who'd have a fit if we stopped traveling. I bet my aunt knows that.

The pills she gave me helped so much that by the time we get back to the carnival I feel good enough to get in the tank and perform for a while.

"But you're still having, um..." says Dad.

"I'm okay," I say. "Not as achy as usual." And my aunt bought a box of tampons for me. Even though I'm in the water all afternoon, I can't hold my breath for more than five minutes. I'm distracted, thinking about what my aunt said. Does Dad not want me to go to college? I never have much homework and my lessons aren't regular, just when he feels like teaching. Usually I don't mind, but I haven't thought a lot about what might happen in a couple years. This could be part of Dad's plan to keep me on the road with him for as long as he can.

Dad is grumpy in the evening because my performance was off. "You weren't concentrating," he says. "You might as well not perform if you can't concentrate."

"I was thinking about this fall," I say. "I need to enroll in school. We need to stop traveling for a while."

"Why?" he says. "You're doing just as good as any kid at your age level, and you're getting a much better education in history and geography."

"But we're doing what you want to do," I say. "What if I want to go to high school for a year? I need to know if I can get into college. We can't do this forever."

This is nothing that I haven't hinted at before, but he doesn't listen.

"When you get older you're going to thank me that you weren't confined to a classroom with all of those robots spitting out answers on multiple choice tests," he says.

"You always use that same damn argument," I say. "I don't believe it anymore. We need to have a year off. You need to get a real job. If you can't handle a real job, you should probably get into therapy or something. Hell, you should probably be in therapy now, not dragging me all across the county."

My father stares at me for a moment. "Don't swear at me," he says very quietly.

This is when I breeze out of the room and run down to the motel pool. My swimsuit's under my clothes. I strip off my shirt and shorts and sit poolside. Water always calms me even though I'm not a great swimmer. We've never stayed in one place long enough for me to take lessons for more than a few weeks.

Dad doesn't follow me to the pool, but I didn't think he would. He doesn't like to argue, and probably figures my outburst is due to hormones and I need time to cool off. But I know this serious problem isn't going to go away.

There aren't many people at the pool, just me and a boy doing laps. After a moment I slip in the water, go under to see him from a different angle. I watch for five minutes, surface when he stops swimming and stands in the water fifteen feet away from me.

"You were under water that whole time?" he says.

I nod.

He lets out a low whistle. He doesn't ask how long I can hold my breath and he doesn't ask me to do it again, which I like. He says his name is Jeremy. We take a couple steps closer and shake hands. It feels adult though we both have wrinkled, cold fingers.

He says he's from St. Paul.

I tell him about holding my breath at the state fair, how Dad and I travel.

"That would be awesome," he says.

"But I don't get to be a high school student," I say.

"It's boring," he says. "You're shut up in a room all day taking stupid classes."

I could tell him that he sounds like my dad, but I don't. Instead we talk about music we like and movies that he's seen and I haven't because Dad hates theaters.

Around ten we towel ourselves off and walk to a little ice cream shack a block from the hotel. Jeremy buys me a cone. There are a bunch of other high school kids there, but I don't know what to say to anyone. Usually when I talk with boys there is water around. I can duck under if things get uncomfortable.

Jeremy's hand is cool and sticky when he holds mine as we walk back to the hotel. We split up in the elevator because his family is on the second floor and Dad and I are on the third.

"See you," says Jeremy. My stomach feels like it's in free fall, floaty and happy and like I might throw up.

When I get back to the hotel room, Dad is sleeping on his bed on top of the comforter, fully clothed. I go into the bathroom, close the door, and start running water in the tub because I want to wash the chlorine out of my hair.

He doesn't even knock, barges through the door right after I've gotten into the tub.

"Where were you?" he yells louder than you should yell in a hotel. "It's after midnight."

"I got back a half hour ago," I say.

"And you didn't wake me?" His face is bright red.

"I thought you'd gone to sleep for the night."

"How could I sleep without knowing where you were? I looked all over the damn hotel."

"I met this guy and we went out to get some ice cream," I say. "That was it."

"A guy?" says Dad. "What have I told you about going out with boys you don't know?"

He hasn't told me anything about going out with boys I don't know, just never to go out with boys in general.

"What if I want to go home and hang out with guys and be in some stupid conventional school?" I say. "What if I don't want to be on the road forever?"

I duck under because I don't want to hear his answer.

Dad grabs me by the shoulder and tries to haul me up, but can't muster the energy. He's not a big guy, and he's kind of tired. He slumps against the tub, the sound of his body amplified through the white porcelain. I lie underwater for a while. It's not as interesting as when I'm performing. There's just the white ceiling and the white walls of tub. No sound of the outside carnival. No barkers selling ride tickets. No one waiting for me to perform.

Dad sits up, turns around, dips both of his hands in the water and lays them on my head. I feel them through my hair, his fingers slightly warm. It's like a blessing. Or like he's trying to drown me. I look at his eyes. They are still mad, dark. I can't tell how hard he is pressing, if he will let me come up. What if he doesn't? For a moment my heart beats too quickly and I can't do it any more, lose my concentration and the rest of my oxygen. I rise and gasp.

My father shakes water droplets from his hands.

"What was that for?" I say, slightly breathless.

"Your hair feels really nice under water," Dad says, his voice cracking. He puts his hand on my hand and doesn't say anything else.

I stand up and grab a white motel towel, slide on my sandals and walk out the bathroom door, then out the motel room door, still dripping. I'll have to call a doctor in the morning, get them to adjust his medications again. I'll have to call my aunt, tell her I'm going to stay with her for a week or two. I don't know if I'll tell her what happened with Dad. I don't know if he'll want to stay with her, too.

I want to sit by the pool but it closed at eleven, so I have to sit on a plastic chair outside the door and stare at the too-blue water. My hips ache. I should have asked my aunt what kind of medication she gave me, but I can find out in the morning. ■

Flood
Ruth Goring

Cacarica Community
Chocó, Colombia

We all went to church that night,
a Tuesday, as a rainstorm walloped
the new zinc roof. Candle flames
shuddered among shadows cast
by a kerosene lamp. Hymns rose
from the dark rows of chairs,
prayers flinched and dodged
the pounding, swam
toward each amen.
We dripped, strained, sang
and Javier loomed in the back
under his great cape.

Clatter cacophony
rain hullabaloo rain rain—
it is too large, Lord,
we will be smithereens.

The rain is hammers.
The rain is *chirimía*.
The rain is hoofbeats of angry mules.
The rain is a wailing river.
The rain is machine gun fire.
The rain is the clamor of mothers.
The rain is fists beating on a door.

The rain is helicopter blades.
The rain is chainsaws.
The rain is testimony.
The rain is a thousand hearts pounding.
The rain is the forest gasping.

The rain is a roll call of the dead
as Javier stands sentry with his
angel face.

Ride
Ruth Goring

Tayrona National Park, Colombia

Though the sky has collapsed in overwrought theatrics,
upends great tanks of tears and cannot catch its breath,
though the path crazy-switches through rock-stubbed foothills,
lurches down bouldered ravines, slumps stone-faced, then
crumples into mud; though you,

not a practiced rider, wear a bulging bedraggled pack
and in its depths your notebooked poems may well
be washing into ink-run oblivion,

                              you loosen the reins.
The creature under your legs' curve—intelligence
of ribs and lungs and shining hide, and hooves'
sure memory—finds her way.

                     The sky sobs its hot joy;
over the hills, the gray sea churns. "Eh-*yah!*" shouts the driver
and you laugh at the mule's sudden canter. Your drenched
and giddy body is hers.

Reading By Riverlight

Jennifer Atkinson

Fluster and scuff, upwell and downshift, all motion the Gihon surface
crimps, crams, rucks, and scars — on the skids, at a slant, on the sly.

Alongside a tangle at silt-edge of jetsam, a water-built scree
of this, that, and the other, quick or decaying, resisting the drag downstream;

West out of Eden, the river's a clean slate, erased and erasing,
doodled on, scratched at, chalked up with practice strokes and aimless

curlicues in readiness for what comes, nothing or — no —
nothing *and* floodwash (snowmelt, downpour) the onrush of visible things.

~ ~ ~

She called it "The Nostalgia of the River Gihon," her green encaustic field,
scratched through to show the clay and sulfur underwork.

I'd have thought the river felt the reverse, the way the current
turns out its pockets, divesting itself of objects, precious and used-up alike,

offering up all it owns to its shores, renouncing all but get-on-with-it.
I mean you don't see the river turning back in regret,

or not going on about its business. What would you call it then,
she said, going over and over the same ground — rehearsal?

~ ~ ~

Nothing needs my attention. I give it, though, anyway
in the four, the six, the ten directions, but especially through

this morning the doorframe window: eavemelt, frozen rain,
a bush strung up with vine and pods swinging a little

in a little wind. Beyond, toward the river, what I take to be
(kinked, crooked, lichened) a crabapple tree, five pines

just askant and a crow flying crosswise. As the crow flies,
the mountains are wearing away.

~ ~ ~

The way the noise has of blurring, clash and sprayfall, drip and slosh,
to one ongoing roar, louder when you look its way or stop seeing *river*
   altogether.

Notice how noticing the culvert spill foregrounds its high-pitched impact,
how calling the slide of water over what's left of the dam *lyric*

sets aside for that strain in the music, a near silence, a sound like rubbed
   suede.
Watch close enough the downwardness of, the dissolve

of snowfall into the largo dark and you'll hear it, the prick and unstitch
of the cold river's seams, the scatter sound of needles dropping.

~ ~ ~

Fog moved over the face of the river, its breath on the pebbled beach
turned overnight to hoarfrost — twigs, asters, sphagnum tufts

of not-quite-snow or ice, minute branchings and interbranchings
as fine as eyelashes, a simulacrum composed in darkness

as if of fingernail parings and strands of white hair. Far too fragile
for close inspection, one touch, one exhalation, returns —

breath for breath — the fog's creation to amorphous drops,
inseparable from the general flood of early winter.

~ ~ ~

Tracks through first snow to the river: Which is what I can't say
— deep powder obscures all but the destination. These deep prints

nagging at my heels are evidently mine, but those I crossed
that stop at the tree might be a squirrel's or a marten's, those

spread out dents and drags could be a cottontail, running. That trail
might be fox-made or as likely a beagle's, off leash and glad to be gadding
     about.

A record of nothing unusual. Just the marks we make by moving —
selving and selving — one (or two) feet in front of the other(s).

~ ~ ~

Before first light, she lay a plank across the thin ice — too thin by noon
to hold up a sparrow — and from that scaffold, on the river erected

cattail-stalk beams, each frozen in steady, and quickly (the sun was rising)
built a rough narthex of briar and sticks, a rush sort-of steeple and door.

The hardest part was removing the scaffold. Her chapel on the river
lasted all of half an hour before the beams listed and toppled,

the steeple and arches reverted to flotsam. I wonder, she said, how I'd feel
if I'd asked you to photograph it — even that silly frill of a steeple.

~ ~ ~

If the river rose from its bed.
If the cloud sank down like a wizened balloon.

Air over the surface hums,
The resonant drone of an open string.

If the fish moon slipped from the sky.
If the flock ascended like a single bird.

Loose pollen and spore, the dust off a winter moth's wings.
A low wind so far barely breathing.

~ ~ ~

Under the valley runs a marble seam; marble, old symbol of perdurance
despite its molten, morphic provenance — fossil coral and bone dust,

salts, eroded, decayed, crushed and entwined, twinned, tripleted,
pressed into lime, refired to liquid, a viscous brook flowing up

through the green flesh of what's become the Green Mountains,
themselves uptilted, thrust-faulted, glaciered over,

and rivered down to valley, this valley, where walking the snowmobile trail
out of town we kick up rocks marbled with marble like meat with fat.

~ ~ ~

Ice starts back over the shallows, a gravel bar where the river slows
to flatten the curve, the current lazy and hurried both,

easing into an oxbow, caps and recaps the stones —
gloss on gloss, a liquid to gelid history of cold

through which the midrashic river slips on underneath
re-emerging darker downstream — creased and pleated,

infolding to fit a rapids its own motion formed,
forms, and over the rocks, works all at once to unform.

Taps on the Forehead
Scott Gould

USED TO BE, wasn't a thing between me and this river but a few big knothole widow maker trees and swamp and cypress knees and wasn't a thing living here but a couple raccoon families in the knotholes and a wild hog I could hear rooting most mornings with his nose down in the mud and his ass cranked up in the air. Two hot summers in a row, and the swamp changed like swamps will do when they left on their own. Dried-up mud and junk weed and stinking like a hot dump. But it was still a quiet place and I could hear that hog hunting for a mud hole deep enough to cool off his nuts. One day it ain't quiet. Some man buys up a chunk of riverfront and stakes out the foundation of a house with a little pissant hammer so brand-new it shines.

He drives a green car with a sticker on the bumper that tells him where to park. I hate shit such as that. Stickers that tell you what you got to do or what you can't do. I got nothing against a sticker of the US of A flag or a Bible verse or something like that, but people showing off parking stickers with numbers on them, they think they better than other people. They think they worth more 'cause they got a space all to their own.

I stand behind a pine at the back corner of my place, and I watch him study a piece of paper spread on the hood of that car. He pulls a measuring tape out his pocket and walks off some distance, then sticks a stake in the ground. He stretches a string tight between another stake and before the afternoon is half over, he's laid out a house among the trees. It doesn't look like much of a house. Looks like some big ass cat's cradle. But it's enough to piss me off, him standing there seeing stuff in his head that's gonna mess up my life.

He's got a German shepherd that follows him around like a toy on a pull string. The dog catches wind of me, sticks his nose in the air and bristles his back in my direction, but sticker man don't even turn. "Hush, baby, now" is all he says. I can hear him good 'cause there ain't twenty feet between me and him and that dog.

So, he's gonna build him a house.

I got no need for a house. I got my trailer. I bought it from a fellow after it'd been burned. Just on one side. Big fucking deal. Looking at it made me think of a potato that somebody forgot to turn. Cost me four hundred dollars, and I had to tow it here myself. But I did it all on my own and it's up on cement blocks now so it don't tilt over when the ground gets soft. I have lived in it for going on four and a half years now, and I have been happy as I can expect. In summer, I open the windows at both ends of the trailer and a breeze blows through the screens all night long. Sounds like a sewing machine running. In winter, I shut everything up tight and stuff pillows under the doorjambs and along the window frames, turn on the kerosene heater, and it gets so warm, I break a sweat before daylight.

I got a trailer, I got a mailbox out by the road, and I got enough space around me, I can walk out on the little two-step porch buck naked if I want to and take me a whiz on the cement blocks. It's different now. There's a man with a dog between me and the river.

"Hey," I say and step out from around my tree. Damn German Shepherd shows me his teeth. Dogs don't never waste time showing you how they feel. Most honest motherfuckers in the world.

"Well, hello," sticker man says, dropping the string and stakes and hammer and putting out his hand, like shaking hands is gonna make us best buddies. Fuck him. "Taylor McElveen," he says, his hand floating there like a bird on the wind. His fingers are blue from the chalk line he been stringing. "Just bought this place. Just doing some preliminary things today. Beautiful land here, huh? God. I think I'll take down some of these trees today. Open things up a bit." He lets a long breath out. A couple of mosquitoes dogfight around his ears.

He's so damn happy you'd think he got laid. I don't trust people who got to use a last name for their first name. I leave his hand hanging til he pulls it back. That smile on his face starts to twitch a little. "And you are ...?" he asks me and reaches down and pats his dog on the head.

"I'm the man come to tell you to keep that dog off my land." I show my teeth a little, especially to the dog. So he'll know I own a set too.

"Pardon?"

"I got a shotgun," I say. The man smiles. Him and his dog must brush their teeth at the same time. He talks low and calm and bats at one of the mosquitoes.

"Oh, now, Fritz is a gentle fellow. He wouldn't hurt anyone. Even you. He never bothers a soul. No need to talk about guns and animals."

"You just keep in mind," I say and his smile goes away like somebody walked up and erased it from a chalkboard.

"Now, look here—" He runs out of patience. I know I'm winning when that happens.

I say, "I ain't gotta *look* at nothing I don't want to and I don't want to look at no dog or no new house or nobody stomping around so close to my trailer. And I'm going to take a nap, so don't start up no chainsaw." I can see the man turn into somebody different right in front of me, which is good. Folks don't like to change on the spur of the moment.

"So you're the guy in the trailer," he says, peering over my shoulder to see it. It's stuck back in the woods though. Can't see it til you walk up on it. It blends good like it belongs there. "I've heard about you."

Sonuvabitch. I'd love to know what people say about me. The only person I know of stupid enough to talk about me behind my back is Sheila, my wife until she decided she'd had enough of the two of us. She has spent the last two years waiting on tables, trying to forget who I am. Her problem is, she can't forget who she is—an ex-wife who's getting bigger and older and works for tips from mill workers and sheriff's deputies who ain't got nothing better to do than drink iced tea and rub up against a filled-out woman in a waitress suit.

Every chance she gets, she shovels people an earful of what a worthless dickhead I am. When them stories eventually float down the river to where I am, I try to shut her up, but every time I go near her, she screams and holds up her waitress ink pen like a little knife, then the cook calls the sheriff and the sheriff shows up and I swear to fucking God them two ought to be married as much as they see one another. She cries on his shoulder and I seen him flex up his muscles so she'll think he is a strong man who can whip me with one hand tied behind a waitress.

But this sticker man won't quit talking. I wonder if he's nervous. "I heard you lived in this area and that you would be by to check out just exactly who I was and what I was up to. Well, I already told you who I am. And what am I up to? I'm up to building a house. My house on my land, accompanied by my dog, who by the way, is very well trained, if you know what I mean." He tries to give me a look like he's tough, tries to make his eyes go hard like ol' Clint Eastwood and make his breath come in puffs, but you can look at his hands and tell he ain't tough at all. Under the blue dust, they soft and white as little pillows. I'll bet he sleeps on his hands. Bet he uses lotion on them.

"You ain't gonna build no house here," I tell him.

"Just watch me," he says.

"I aim to, mister," I say which I think sounds like it came from a movie, it sounds so good. Clint Eastwood. I can do Clint better than Clint can. It sounds like I ain't scared of anything short of a bolt of God's lightning. He just stares at his hands when he hears me, but I walk off before he has a chance to answer good. Ten minutes later, he's packed up and gone back where he came from, and I flip a bird at his dust.

~ ~ ~

Next morning, Raymond's at my door, banging it so his high school ring hits on the wood strip. I see his Ford idling through the window.

"I ain't gone near Sheila!" I yell at the door.

"Yeah, but you went and bothered that guy building the house."

"So?"

"Ain't too neighborly of you."

"I don't want no neighbors," I say. We're doing all of this through the door.

"You ain't got a choice. He bought the land. He can do what he wants on it, within reason, you know. Now, if you keep on with him, I'm gonna have to take you into town."

I can't say a thing. That may be true about his land, but I ain't gotta like it. "For what? Ain't a law in the land against speaking your piece. That's covered in the pledge of allegiance or something."

Raymond stops for a second because he knows I got a point, then he goes on. "You leave him alone, hear? Let him build his house. And don't you so much as think about taking target practice on his dog. Anyway, you ain't supposed to have a gun, what with your parole."

Parole. Shit. About the most confusing thing the world can do to a man is stick his ass on parole. I can't never remember what I'm supposed to do or not do on parole. If you sit the wrong way on the commode, they haul you in for breaking parole. They's so many rules, makes me feel like I'm back in high school.

Sheila had a date one night with some pretty boy right after we split up, and I ended up beating the guy's head in. I didn't want to beat him so bad, but he kept laughing when I hit him. I wanted to make him stop laughing. He didn't die, which was good, but Sheila won't never go out with him again because he left town after they let him out of the hospital. He didn't look the same. Eighteen months, aggravated assault. And then that damn parole. When I got back to the trailer, there was a whole group of possums living in the kitchen. I ate every one them greasy fuckers the first week I was out of jail.

"Ain't even got so much as a water pistol. I was just talking. Can't hurt nobody with just words."

"Well, you can sure scare the shit out of them. You just leave him be."

"Fine," I say and nod my head which he can't see.

"Fine and dandy," he says back and walks off the porch. "I better not hear about any goddamn gun," he yells over his shoulder.

~ ~ ~

My daddy always called me the worst kind of pest. *You make people crazy*, was what he said. What I really do is make people do things they feel bad about the next day. I've made school teachers run right out the door, hit their knees and cry in the hall until the bell rang. I've made cousins claim we ain't kin. I've made women swear they never laid eyes on me.

It's a secret, knowing how to make people crazy. The secret is, it ain't no big thing. You don't have to hit people over the head with a hammer to make them crazy. You just got to tap them on the forehead with a pencil about six hundred times in a row. What I'm saying is, you ain't got to be strong or quick. You just got to be mean and stay at it. That's the whole thing about it.

I go over after dark the next day, after him and his dog've left and I stand there looking at the string he spent all afternoon stretching. It shines like spider web in the light my old Coleman lantern throws off. I can't decide whether to move the stakes a little or just cut the string. I do both. I pile the stakes in the middle of his invisible house and ball up the leftover string. Then I start me a bonfire that ain't all that big, but it gets hot enough and makes the trees look like they alive and dancing. I cut off my Coleman lantern to save on fuel and I feel like an Indian or something—dancing with my shadow around a fire.

Next morning, I'm squatting in the trees doing my private business when he pulls up and looks at the pile of black coals in the middle of his land. He sticks his neck out like a bird toward my direction, unclips his dog from a leash and starts staking up his house again. He don't even think about it, just starts right up with the measuring and pounding. No cussing or anything. It takes him until the middle of the afternoon to get the first bunch of lines pulled. It turns hotter and the gnats come out. He has sweat all the way through one t-shirt and took it off, and now he's turning pink, slapping at the bugs on his bare back. He won't last here long; neither will that dog of his if it keeps walking the edge of my property, that long limp dick tongue of his hanging pink out his mouth.

Seeing the two of them working so hard makes me thirsty, so I decide to take the truck to town. I ain't worried. He wouldn't dare fuck with me or my stuff. He's too nice for that. I got a craving for a beer and a Chocolate Soldier. I started drinking the two of them together when I was still in high school. Out in the parking lot during lunch, I'd have me a bottle of Chocolate Soldier in my hand and a cold beer tucked behind my back. Sip the Soldier when the teacher came walking by. Sip the beer when the coast was clear. The taste grew on me.

Stimey keeps me a case of Chocolate Soldiers behind the bar. Usually sees me coming and has me set up by the time I hit the door. Inside The Cotton Bottom, they no light bulbs in the light sockets and the air's so thick, it's like walking into spider webs. The only glowing comes from the juke box and the neon Miller High Life sign that buzzes behind Stimey's bar.

He starts talking to me before my eyes get used to the dark. "Sheila says you about to step on your pecker again, says you gonna end up slow-dancing with some fudge-packer down at county."

I ain't took my first sip yet and he's already fucking with me. I hate bartenders.

"Messing with that professor the way you do," he says. "Lord, lord ..."

"Professor?"

"What bought the land next to yours."

"Professor?"

"At the college. The girl's school."

"I seen them girls before."

"He teaches history, somebody said."

"He a fag?"

"No, just a professor."

"How do you know all this?"

"Son, if I don't hear it first hand, then I hear it from somebody who heard it first hand. Sheila told me all about the professor. She waits on him at the diner. Sheila says you're an idiot. Says you gonna wind up in jail where you belong."

The Chocolate Soldier is empty, and there's only a sip of beer left. Stimey ducks down to grab another round. "I quit caring about what Sheila says," I tell him.

"Yeah, like hell you don't."

"Fuck you."

"Ain't me we talking about. And I'm the only one who can talk like that in my place, so shut up. You want a glass?" He knows I don't never use a glass, but he's just trying to get another rise out of me.

It turns dark outside while I drink and drink and don't pee and get a buzz on so good I think I can catch bullets or dodge cars, one of those you-can't-kill-me buzzes. I walk by the diner and there's Sheila through the window, smiling while she pours coffee, bending over and stretching her blue uniform on the backside. She doesn't see me, which is good. When I am drunk, I don't win none of the arguments I start.

Behind the diner, in the gravel parking lot, I find her Plymouth Duster. I want to leave her something, so she'll know I been there and know I could've made a scene. If I had paper, I could leave a note. Her car is backed into a parking space, with enough room between the bumper and the wall for me to pee. When I ain't weaving and blocking the light from the telephone pole, I see she's got a goddamn parking sticker, just like the Professor. I keep moving in and out of the light, so the sticker looks like it's blinking at me. Winking at me. I hate stickers. I hate it that Sheila has one. Through that window, she didn't look as fat as she used to be. I hate that too. If she goes and messes around and gets happy, I'm liable to kill somebody. I end up pissing all over my shoes.

The sticker won't peel off, so I break off both of her windshield wipers, snap them free like they was dead twigs. I shove them up her tailpipe. The next time it rains, I hope she goes blind trying to find the fucking road.

~ ~ ~

He heard my truck leave. Fucker. Heard me leave and figured I wouldn't be back for a long time. That was a gamble. I could have been just going to the store.

While I was gone, he cut down a dozen trees round his house site, it looks like, then walked his dog right up on my little two-step porch and let him drop a load. He did say that his dog was trained, *if I know what he means.*

That dog's been eating well. Leaves a pile of shit so big, you'd swear a cow'd been running around my trailer. Leaves it right where I'll step in it too. I see it before I smell it, but what with all the beer and Chocolate Soldiers, my piss-smelling feet is under their own control. Right smack in it, like stepping into mud. When I was a kid, we had a big old hunting dog that used the whole backyard as his private shithole. We'd step in stuff all day long. Never bothered me then, and if he thinks it bothers me now, he's dumber than I thought. He may know history, but he don't know mine. I just leave my shoes in the yard and go to sleep. In the morning, everything will be dry and easy to scrape off with a kitchen knife.

~ ~ ~

I sleep through the next morning until I think my head quits hurting. I hear him out there, banging stakes and whistling to his dog every once in awhile. Sometimes, I think I'm dreaming. My stomach feels like I sucked down drain opener. Sometimes the beer and the chocolate don't mix good. Inside of my mouth feels like it has hair growing in it. I'd slap my grandma for a big coke with crushed ice right now. If I was with Sheila, she'd bring it to me in bed. She would do little things like that.

The banging stops and an engine starts up. I think it might be one of them weed whacker things until the sound moves up the road. It's his car. He's gone and he left by himself, because when I peek out the window of my trailer, I can see that dog, walking back and forth along the property line like he is a freaking Marine. He don't never take his eye off my trailer, and when I go out on the back steps in my underwear, he stops walking the whole time I'm peeing. Them ears are up and cocked back just a little.

"Squirrel butt!" I yell toward him, and he just sits and sniffs the air. He never stops looking.

I take an old lawn chair from under the trailer and put in out in front, and me and that dog watch each other for an hour. I sweat beer and chocolate and smell like the inside of a boot, but the only reason I leave my chair is to get a new beer. I didn't have no coke in the refrigerator. And what with the sun and the beer, pretty soon I got an encore buzz on. I just wish I had a Chocolate Soldier or two. I try tricking the dog with niceness, calling out to him and smacking my lips, trying to get him to come in the yard for a little kiss, but he ain't having none of it.

I shut my eyes when the sun gets up high and I have a foggy dream about that dog. I dream he comes tiptoeing across the line and sniffs at the bottoms of my feet, then starts licking my toes, which don't feel too bad, just tickles some when his tongue keeps flicking around my foot and my ankle. Makes me twitch. The dog is smiling at me, like he's going to tickle me to death.

I start laughing in my sleep so hard from the dream-tickling that I wake up and when I look down, I see I got a whole goddamn army of fire ants making their way up my leg. The minute I jump out the chair, they get mad and start biting and before I can get to the hose pipe and wash them off, they done bit into most of the hide on my leg all the way up to the knee. It hurts so bad the only thing I can do is throw up and that dog never takes his eyes off me the whole time.

When the sun starts going down behind the trees, I've still got the sweats from all the ant bites but they feel better since I rubbed the Karo syrup all over them. It's that dog's damn fault I got stung five million times. I got lessons to show him.

My fishing rod is under the porch. It's rigged with forty pound test line that looks like steel wire and's so strong I could pull over small trees with it. In the bottom of my tackle box, in amongst all the split shot and pieces of rubber worms, I got a good size treble hook, maybe a number six or something. I tie it on my line and bury it deep inside a piece of leftover hamburger steak I find in the frigerator. The dog ain't got no idea. Probably thinks I'm going catfishing or something.

I move my chair closer to the property line and make sure I ain't setting up over an ant hill. I get close enough to drive that dog crazy. Don't want to make him mad because with my leg the way it is, I couldn't run from anything. I check my reel, then flip the piece of meat in his direction. He backs up a few steps in the dirt. I flip it again and again, a couple of feet closer each cast. He wants to know what it tastes like. He wants to know bad. He looks at me, then at the meat, then at me. He can't make up his mind.

Finally, I'm tossing it right in front of him. It's almost dark now. He's seeing with his nose. I know he ain't eaten all day, unless he snuck off while I was sleeping. He wants to know. The light is getting bad. I can hear the meat hit the ground, but I lose sight of it in the air. I'm getting close, I know. I am a patient man. I been fishing all my life and I ain't found a bass yet that can outwait me.

He sniffs one of my casts. I can barely see his nose right on it. I'm talking to him, the same way I talk to the fish when I'm in the river. "Go 'head, sonuvabitch, you hungry, you know you hungry. Big bite." He sniffs and walks away. I reel in the meat, check the hook and toss again. He can't stand it.

This time he picks up the meat and carries it real soft, like he's holding an egg in his mouth, and he starts walking toward the center of the property. I give him plenty of line. The meat's still in his teeth. Just like a damn fish. Got to go get some privacy before he can eat. Can't bring hisself to chew in public. I can barely make out his shape. He stops and puts the meat on the ground. Watches it for a second. I twitch the line. Then he gobbles it, throws his head back and sucks it down his throat.

He knows right away he's fucked. He starts running for the woods, not making no noise, and the line is zipping off my reel, sounds like a mad beehive. I'm still patient. "I'm gonna break your fucking back," I tell him. "I'm gonna jerk your stomach through your fucking teeth." I let him take line 'til I'm down to the last fifty feet or so, and I plant my heels in the dirt, throw the drag and snatch that dog blind from the goddamn pain.

He howls like a ghost. The drag don't even slow him down, so I tighten it. I ain't worried about the line breaking. That's why I use forty pound test. The line goes slack. He's back-tracking on me. "Just like a goddamn bass!" I scream, reeling as fast as my wrist will move. I take out the slack and set the hook again, and I can see him now, running circles in the property, rolling on his back, cutting flips in the air. I feel like I'm on a goddamn fishing show. He's howling, wishing he was dead. I got the butt of the rod between my legs, and the thing is bent over like fucking pulp wood in a hurricane. The dog takes off for the woods again. I know he ain't hooked in the lip 'cause he ain't shaking his head, trying to throw it out. That damn hook is grinding away inside his stomach by now. About the time he hits the trees, he ain't nothing but a shadow. I take out my pocket knife and cut him loose. He'll die tonight, bleeding from the inside out, and that'll be the last time somebody puts a dog on their property to keep an eye on me. Goddammit.

~ ~ ~

"I ain't been outside this trailer since yesterday morning. Since them ants tried to carry me off." I pull my pants leg up and Raymond squints his eyes. He's been bit before hisself so he knows what it looks like.

"You oughta watch where you step. Looks like you been hit with number nine shot."

"I fell asleep in my chair," I say.

"He ain't seen his dog since yesterday morning. I told him I got a coon dog that stays out weeks at a time chasing nookie, but he said his wouldn't do that kind of thing. He says he told the dog to stay in the yard and the dog does everything he says to." Raymond don't really care. I can see it in his eyes. The man next door is starting to get on his nerves. The professor is starting to turn into a pain in the ass. Raymond wishes he'd go away, too.

"Well, I'm sure glad you taking care of this, Raymond. I'm glad there ain't nothing more important to do than this. Fuck all them gangs and rapers and car thiefs. Did I miss it or they make you dog catcher too?"

"You shoot that dog?" he asks me, but he don't care.

"Shot him and ate him for supper. Tough fucker. Hard to chew. I got some leftovers inside. You had lunch?" I smile.

"You so damn funny. It ain't gonna be so funny if you did something to that guy's dog. He's pretty pissed right now."

I feel my heart beating a little faster, but I ain't about to let anybody know it. "And what's he gonna do? Come over here and whip my ass? Hell, only thing he can whip is his own dick."

Raymond digs around in his ear with the key to his police car. He looks tired. "Why you got to be like this?"

"Like what?"

"Like such trash. All you got left in your life is a bad attitude. You wasn't like this before Sheila left. You need to get you somebody, if that's what'll keep you from being such trash. Find you a woman. Or buy a TV set or something. Move on in life."

Raymond always works her into a conversation, one way or the other. "You think Sheila's my problem? Says who? Sheila? She ain't nothing to me. You see, Raymond, you start believing everything that woman says, you'll end up like me. Goddamn, she's just like a weathergirl on TV. She says something and everybody believes it."

"I hope you didn't hurt that dog."

"I hope that dog and that man die slow and turn into maggot food."

"I'll be back. I'll be sure and tell Sheila you're about the same as always. She asks about you, you know. And sometimes she really wants to know how you doing."

That stops me a little. Just knowing that she even thinks about me makes my breath short. I back into the door without saying a word and lie down on the floor where it's a little cooler. When I close my eyes, Sheila is swimming there, in the air, in some place where there ain't no stars or clouds, stripping her waitress clothes off until she's bare-assed naked and sweating, shining and floating in front of my eyes like a bird. She talks to me through the air and I see each one of her words come popping out of her mouth like soap bubbles and they *plink!* when they hit my ear, her telling me she wants to come back, wants me to do whatever I want and she wants to do things to me she don't even know how to do. She licks my ear and unzips my jeans and tells me I'm gonna be too big for her, but I take her right there. I'm laying on the floor, watching me do it, with my eyes closed, curling up my toes and banging my head on the floor of my burned out trailer, jerking off like some high school boy who can't get laid anywhere but in his own mind's eye these days.

~ ~ ~

They never find the dog, but he knows I did it. He knows 'cause all I do is wave at him now while he digs the footings for his house. I am too friendly. I call him "neighbor" out loud and on purpose, and he ain't said a word to me in three weeks. He had some men out to clear the rest of the trees, and now he works on the house in the afternoons, until dark, then he climbs in his car and drives off.

I don't even go over there when he's gone. I know I could fill in his holes and cut his string or stomp in his wet cement, but I'm driving him crazy without breaking a sweat. I'm tapping him on the forehead with that pencil. Me, the pest. I ain't been to town. I been keeping my hands out of my pants. I feel like a new person because I'm winning this fight even though a house is going up, and when I'm winning, I don't need anything else in the world from anybody.

On Sunday night, he comes driving back to his land around ten o'clock. It's something different for him, being around that late at night. From inside my trailer, I see the headlights bouncing through the trees and when he turns the car off, there's music still playing loud, making thumping noises. *Boombaddaboombuddaboom* ... It's country music. He opens the door and the music gets louder, and I see two heads, one of them's a woman, and they're laughing and singing along with the songs they know. He lights a camping lantern and hangs it on one of the two by fours stuck in the ground. They start dancing in the circle of light the thing throws off. When they stop, she ducks inside the car and pulls out a little cooler. The way it sounds, the last thing them two need is another one. At least he ain't a fag. I want to tell him to be careful. Too much of that stuff in the cooler and he won't be able to get it up. I'm almost proud of him, having a woman over there. Makes him more like somebody I could get to know.

The woman pops the top on a beer and hollers at him. "Bottoms up, Big Boy," and my breath catches in my throat like a fish bone. "There ya go!" She's still hollering.

This would be a good time to die. My ears burn. Used to be, *I* was the Big Boy. Big Boy. Sheila called me that all the time. Now I see the curve of her head and hear the way she sings. Sheila is next door, so close I can almost smell her.

I can't see straight. I bang the back door when I sneak out. I gotta hold trees to keep from falling. I got no shoes on. I make it through the woods and finally hug this tree twenty feet from the car and stay out of sight. I got to tell her to shut up. *Don't go calling people names.* She's got her waitressing uniform on, but he's zipping it down, silver flashing in the lantern light.

"BIG BOY!" she says and steps out of it. She takes the rest off while he kicks his shoes into the shadows and pulls down his shorts.

Sheila lays back on the hood of his car, her knees in the air. "Watch out," he says, "the hood might still be hot."

"Shut up," she says and laughs. "Hot's right here." She laughs like she told a decent joke.

He's standing up when he does it. Sheila beats out time on the fenders with her hands. They are both covered with sweat, their heads are a few feet apart but ain't neither one watching the other. She's eyeballing the sky and starts singing along with the radio, her voice chopped up by his pushing. Sounds like she's got hiccups. He shakes his head once and the sweat slings off and sparkles like fireworks when the light catches it in the air.

"Big Boy," she says, and he keeps going on and on, reaching down and hooking his fingers through the grill so he can pull against her. I hear the shocks squeaking on his car. "Professor ..." she hollers.

He starts screaming, but not at her. "NEIGHBOR!" he yells. "HEY, NEIGHBOR!" Motherfucker keeps up for another quarter hour, and I can hear him yelling even though I'm back in the trailer with a pillow over my head and all the windows closed up tight. The sound won't let me be. He must think I won't kill him. I didn't think he had it in him.

~ ~ ~

The next morning it is cloudy but it ain't rained. You can almost feel the water in the air. Raymond pulls up with his lights on. I can see them flashing through windows. He don't knock. He kicks the door like those cops on TV.

"Wake up, you sorry shit-for-brains," he yells through the door. "And bring your goddamn toothbrush. You're going to jail!"

"Get the fuck away from my door!"

"You're such a damn redneck! You're a fucking afterbirth!"

I crack the door and Raymond pushes through. He has his handcuffs out, and he slaps one of them on my wrist. "You got the right to be quiet and you got the right for me to kick your bony ass into next week, you shit stain." He cinches the other cuff before I can even open my mouth to ask what's going on.

"Shut up," he says. "Don't even say a thing. You're moving out."

"For what?"

"For being an ass wipe," he says, steering me toward the door.

Then he waits for me to ask him something else, but to tell you the God's honest truth, I didn't care. I feel warm and happy. Raymond is hauling somebody off, but it ain't me, really. Most of the real me is laying balled up on the floor, thinking of ways to tell Sheila that I don't give a shit about her if she stays miserable, but the second she starts having a good time, I'm in love all over again. Even though she was double-humping the Professor on the hood of his car. Loved her *because* of that. It ain't a jealous thing. It's something that ain't got a name. It's a different kind of being confused.

The real me, the one that don't give a flying fuck about Raymond, is thinking up ways to kill the professor without a sound. I want to think. I got no plans to talk. It is one of the first times in my whole life I decide to shut up. I have other things on my mind, and no handcuffs or sheriff is going to clear my head.

"What you got to say for yourself?" Raymond finally asks me. He can't stand the quiet.

"About what? I ain't done nothing to Sheila. I ain't gone near that Professor!"

"Yeah, what about his dog."

"Dog?"

"The college man's dog. The professor's. I can't believe you. You're such a fuck up."

We are on the porch now. It is so cloudy out that it seems like evening or dawn. I take a breath and spit at the dirt. I ain't thought about that dog in days.

"I'm making you sit right in the wet spot." Raymond steers me again while we walk toward his police car.

"Wet spot? I don't know what you're talking about, Raymond. I ain't done nothing to that dog. He just run off. He got lost. Maybe a snake bit him or a coon drowned him. Don't blame me 'cause the dog got bored and left."

"I don't care about him leaving. What I care about is where he showed back up."

"What?"

"Goddammit, I know playing stupid comes easy for you, but give it up, okay? Just give it up. I can't believe you let that dog rot that way. Did you bury him and dig him up later? And you ruined my fucking back seat. Motherfucker was so full of maggots. I'll probably have maggots in my seat cushions forever. My car will probably take off from all the flies one day. And it'll be a miracle if the smell ever leaves. I been driving around with the windows open."

I start laughing. Throw my head back and let it pour out of my mouth. Raymond tells me once to shut up, then he hits me. I feel my cheek pop inside my mouth, but I keep laughing. Even when Raymond stuffs me in the back seat and pushes my face into the wet, brown stain on the seat, I keep laughing and keep laughing until it don't seem funny anymore, until I feel my breath backing up in my throat and I start choking on my tongue. Raymond is in my ear.

"You puke and I'll make you lay in it," he whispers. So I smile and make sure I keep it all down.

~ ~ ~

I stay in jail for two days. Raymond can't keep me any longer because he can't prove I killed the dog or put him in the police car. I don't know if they found the fish hook or not. Don't matter. A dog could pick up a hook anywhere along the river. Raymond can only get mad as long as the law lets him. He won't even talk to me. I try to catch a ride back out to the river, but there ain't one to be had, so I walk most of the morning and part of the afternoon. The tar on the road smells and shimmies from the heat.

When I round the curve on the river road, I can see the tracks of the heavy trucks. Cement trucks. The Professor is pouring the last footings for his house, leaning against a tree, watching a man in a t-shirt guide the wet cement into the holes. He seems to know when I'm clear of the trees and in plain sight because he turns and smiles at me the whole way into my trailer. I flip him the bird, but it don't do a thing to his smile. There ain't a bit of fear on his teeth. He thinks he won. He is a new man. He thinks piling that stinking lump of a dog into Raymond's car made him the champion, thinks it was such a good trick. All it cost me was a couple of days of free food and decent air conditioning.

They work most of the day, the cement man sweating through his dirty t-shirt and the Professor cutting a path back and forth between the wet footings and his water cooler. By the end of the afternoon, most of the foundation is poured and I'm settling in. I'm ready for the evening. My head is buzzing like a ground hornet.

Like a damn ghost, Sheila appears out of nowhere, in the footprint of the Professor's house. She don't look toward my trailer. She's pretending I'm dead. She don't care one way or the other. I got to pee but I'm too scared to walk outside. She's the only person in the world that makes me act this way.

The Professor takes off his shoe and sticks his foot in the wet cement. Sheila puts her hand in and giggles like she's touched something gross. They both walk down toward the river, to wash off the cement I guess. I can't see that far. I lose them in the trees. I hope he steps on a water moccasin. I hope he steps on one and she has to watch him do it. I wish as hard as I can for a snake. I pray for a snake with a mouth as big as the opening of a Mason jar. But God don't listen to them kind of prayers. You got to be your own kind of God sometimes. That's what I got out of church when I was a kid. You can wait on God to do shit and you might die from boredom or being scared. Or you can do things on your own and let God figure out how to deal with you. Most of the people in hell are people who got things done on their own when they was living.

Be God my own self. That's what I do. I make it look like an accident. I've seen TV shows. Slosh a little kerosene from the heater on the floor and in the mattress. Not much. I find me a cigarette in the drawer, leftover from when Sheila used to be here. I take a couple drags and lay it down on the mattress. Shouldn't been smoking in bed. Bad boy, Big Boy. Everybody knows trailers go up like fat lighter wood.

The mattress is already smoking when I grab my clothes and throw them into a grocery bag. They ain't come back from the river yet. Probably swimming naked. They'll see it soon enough. Glowing like a big old giant lightning bug. As dry as it is, the whole woods will be going before long. I pray for wind. Fan them fucking flames. I'm good, but I ain't good enough to tell the wind what to do.

My truck starts right up even though it ain't been cranked in a few days. The radio works. I turn it up loud. They'll hear the music, some kind of dull thump-thump down at the river. Time to rock and roll. The trailer crackles from heat and the fire climbs up a pine that grows outside the kitchen. The flames get sucked quick into the high limbs. Everything close will burn down. No stopping this fire until it hits the river or the highway. I head my truck up the road, trying to decide which way to turn when I reach pavement. I know without turning around to look; for a couple of years these woods won't be fit for a house, won't be fit for a living thing, not even the damn raccoons.

Salvage
Karen Holmberg

i.

We're safe giving   griefs of any kind
            or scale to something

                so   mutable
where trees   compromise with current's

undercut of bank   by growing out
            narrow docks

                leaf-awninged   over
the water   So full   of digression   so able

to reclaim our prosaic trash   Scummed
            and rainbow-faded   a

                Cheer jug bashed
to brittle shard   mulch fabric

bunched in tree crotches   tar drums
            scraps of raft

                aluminum lawn
chairs   the webbing shredded

snagged   twenty feet up a tree
            A scene enduring   no   enriched

                by calamity
velveted anew each flood in silt   Stress

can make beautiful   what suffering
            lets go of

                I thought the swag
suspended between   two sycamores was tarp

until I noticed   in eroded places
          the narrow slats and cord-like bones

                    of the great   blue heron wings
The slick transcript I'd made

of his desire   for another   not for me
          stumbled upon   hoarded   got

                    by heart   I tore into
strips   then   difficult rungs

                    ~ give yourself ~

                         ~ how I wish ~

     ~ in one ~
                              that spun
their origami moment

                    ~ I only know I am in ~

          ~ such risks ~

                         ~ the courage to insist ~

extended their wings   their euphoria
          subdued   somchow

                    more moving   It was
possible   to confess   I had envied

I had admired them   as they drank
          to a waxed   transparency

                    as they sank
to petals   radium green

ii.

Three days rain   so altered
  the mobile verge   the evidence
     I'd let go   was
          unlocatable
Even the place I'd crouched   had drowned
         in that spacious bed

The river takes all   our sadness or offense
  without reproach   like a girl
  her hymen torn   coming to her door to lean
her cheek against   the frame   lower lids sooted
  sleep   smutched   the apricot under lip
  with the   should-have-been-adored
freckle in its border   Girl   this river
      has your eyes

iii.

When my walks had turned to   blind staggering
in the wastes of our estrangement   the river threw

its lifeline to my eye   On the bank   a pagoda of yellow petals
on a stem   arched just so   that tremble

could go on   A pair of leaves netted with blur- edged
light belied   the trout lily   and not

just one   no   but another linked   another to my eye
nodding   pointing with their chin

       Look

            there is still a world

out here   even if pain
    has made you stupid

iv.

I walk the trunk out over the water   my steps
        shuddering   schools

of silver-bellied leaves   I hold to vertical
        branches strongly jointed   as the hard legs

of horses and look down at the dimpling
        over black stones water   the counterclockwise

of minnows that keep a place by conceding
        to a new one   the cursive of snail trail

a lanky water weed   emerging
        miraculous   unsnagged   from a gamut of branches

                        In the shallows
        a carp flops its sunning self

then shoots off   a muscular kick   conducting
        to my chest   the volts of animal alarm

Herds of beetles   featureless
        as drops of hot

solder zoom and slalom along the surface   colliding
        like electrons   taking momentum from that push

A view's made possible by a bearable
        duress   by roots feeling out

what anchorage there is   within a shifting bank
        Whatever   happens becomes

part of this beauty   will be incorporated
        in the growth pattern over time.

Nocturne with Mysterious Leak
Matthew Nienow

Water's running down the wall
to the floorboards, making

a bad stain, a warping of the wood, a rotting—

and the white paint is growing fat with water,
brown runs like banks of a distant river, no depth

to the run, so it's like a map of what's happened.

Everything has been pushed to the middle of the room
like a raft of upholstery in a pond of wood.

A lamp flickers and goes out. A pale light creeps

through the glass and you climb onto the raft and listen
to the patter grow to a heavy hushing, a song of *nothing*

can be done and so you do nothing,

just captain the couch flotilla, drifting off,
charting the flooded country of

this room named for the living.

Spring Thaw

Matthew Nienow

And then I thought, what happens around
the bend doesn't stay around the bend,
it's only a matter of being upstream
or down, fat logs water heavy from a winter
of bobbing in the icy current, until
breakup in the lakes above makes the water
rise quickly, a foot in an hour, the urge
of *more* being forced through *less*,
the current corralling debris in a stampede
that stops only for islands & bridge abutments,
these pilings rising to a story-high instability,
or tossed over the edge of a low-head dam
to spin in the unbroken hydraulic,
as the water reaches back over itself,
sometimes battering whole trunks against
the wall. The river is trying to take
down the dam. And of course, this draws
the onlookers, because who isn't amazed
by a forty foot tree being tossed through the air,
only to rise over and over; and the deep rumbling
concrete, the wrought iron ringing,
the wood discolored with rot, two or three
times more burdened with weight—
it should mean something, this
fight against the current.

The Inner Circle

Matthew Nienow

I'd seen this boy each year tear through
woods with machete, burning
books and benches, illuminating night,
smoke trailing him like a sour ghost,
even in his small boat, the motor giving up
a thin gray cloud—and it was the boat
that made him famous to me. Not
the boat itself, but the way he drove it,
carving deep circumferences in the lake's
still face, angering the quiet, riding
low in the made grooves until he reached
his own wake and went crashing through
it, as though his life weren't turbulent
enough, he needed to remake
what made him. I'm talking about
a boy whose name I never learned.
I wasn't there when from the boat
he was tossed, sent into his own small patch
of violent water, the boat, running
smoothly, still writing circles in the lake
(now red). But it isn't difficult to imagine:
the low moaning of the motor
and how different it sounded,
muffled, whining underwater.

Ships in the Desert
Jeff Fearnside

TWO IMAGES REMAIN with me:

The first is of the Technicolor tile mosaic covering the entire back wall of the waiting room in Aralsk's century-old railway station. Strong men and women, faithfully portrayed in the Soviet realist style, haul in nets teeming with fish and load them onto waiting railway cars. Large Cyrillic script spells out the reason for their industry: "In response to Lenin's letter, let's load fourteen train wagons of fish." The mural is a tribute to the time when Aralsk's citizens helped feed a starving young Soviet nation during a famine. It's a tribute to the life-giving bounty of the Aral Sea.

The second is of a fleet of rusting Soviet fishing ships, hammer and sickle still clearly discernible on many, sitting bolt upright in desert sands as if plowing through ocean waves. At that time, I had already lived for almost a year and would live for another three in beautiful, crazy, haunting, surreal Kazakhstan. But the sight of those ships, so lost no storm could have put them there, so dead and yet so apparently alive, was the most beautiful, the most surreal. The story of how they got there is certainly the most crazy, no small boast in a land of storied fighting, infighting, greed, and corruption. That it has haunted me is why I had to write this.

The Aral Sea disaster is one of the worst human-caused environmental catastrophes of the past century, perhaps the worst. In only four decades, what was the world's fourth-largest inland body of water shrank to a mere 10 percent of its former volume. Average salinity sextupled, and its once flourishing fishing industry was destroyed. Agrochemicals exposed on the dry seabed easily found their way into the surrounding environment; the region's people now suffered from some of the highest rates of cancer and infant mortality in the world. Despite the dramatic scope of all this, like something from a science fiction novel, it's surprising how little-known the disaster remains.

Before the September 11 tragedy and our two subsequent wars, few Americans had even heard of Kazakhstan or Uzbekistan, the two countries that share the sea. Now many have, but only from seeing them at the edges of maps in newspapers or hearing scraps about them in newscasts, between much larger chunks about Afghanistan and Pakistan. My experience has been that most Americans, even those who are educated and well-traveled, confuse all the Central Asian countries with these other two 'stans. Mentioning the Aral Sea doesn't clear the confusion.

Even in Shymkent, Kazakhstan, when I would ask my university students about this disaster taking place in their own country, almost none knew that the sea had become so dried up it had split into two sections. (It has since split into three.) A couple who did know confidently told of a dike project to save the smaller northern portion, or Little Aral—a project that had already failed twice. Shymkent was then only some eight hundred kilometers (five hundred miles) from the sea, but based on the knowledge and interest of the local people, one might have thought the Aral was on another planet.

Sadder yet was hearing of the older generation still living in Aralsk, the former bustling fishing port, who, because the waters had retreated so far away, refused to believe the sea still existed. To them, it hadn't disappeared metaphorically; old villagers in Kazakhstan don't think this way. The sea was physically gone forever. And when looking at the rusting hulls of ships mired in the dry harbor, and then beyond them across windswept sand—the former seabed—stretching all the way to the horizon, who could say they were wrong?

Most importantly, what lessons does the Aral Sea disaster have to teach the rest of the world? Frighteningly, many. It's not the unique result of former Soviet megalomania, shortsightedness, or excess. Until last year, the problem had steadily worsened since the collapse of the Soviet Union, due to the inability of all the countries involved—formerly republics in the same country—to work together. America has its own Aral Sea—several of them, which somehow have failed to generate the attention that might be expected given the serious implications they hold. And widespread lack of potable water may be the most pressing problem for every country on the planet sooner than most currently recognize. If we're not careful, the twenty-first century could well be defined not by terrorism or the growing disparity between rich and poor but by water wars.

I. Cutting through choppy waves

At the beginning, you drink water; at the end, you drink poison.
—Uzbek proverb

In early May 2003, a small group of colleagues and I living in Kazakhstan decided to visit the sea before it disappeared completely. So from the medieval city of Turkistan we hopped aboard an overnight train for a modern nightmare.

Getting to the sea was never easy even before it began shrinking. It lies in the heart of the Eurasian landmass—south of Russia, east of the Caspian Sea, and north and west of the towering mountain ranges that separate Central Asia from China and the Indian subcontinent—surrounded by inhospitable deserts and lonely steppes. For some seventy years, it remained behind the Iron Curtain, inaccessible to foreigners. Though both of its major ports, Aralsk in the north and Muynak in the south, were linked by rail to the rest of the Soviet Union, they were far from any other cities of consequence.

Even before arriving in Aralsk, we could see signs of the disaster right outside our train window. All along the railway, salt covered the sandy earth for scores of kilometers. More troubling, I knew it wasn't just salt but also a dry cocktail of chemicals—fertilizers, pesticides, herbicides, and defoliants—that for decades had washed from farms in the watershed, settled to the bottom of the Aral Sea, and were now being blown with the salt from the naked seabed.

We were met at Aralsk's train station by Jonathan and Leah, Peace Corps volunteers with a Danish-funded NGO project, "From Kattegat to the Aral Sea." When someone commented on all the salt we'd seen, Jonathan replied that recent rains had washed away much of this crust. Still, so much remained that it appeared like a dusting of snow. It was hard to imagine what it must have looked like only a few weeks before. Probably like glare ice.

We breakfasted at Jonathan and Leah's. The meal was simple: instant coffee, flat rounds of *lepyoshka* bread, and *plov*, a Central Asian rice dish. Our hosts explained that it was hard to find much more than this in Aralsk's bazaars and stores. We did, however, find sand in the bread. The crunch was startling. Grinding against one's teeth, the grains feel larger than they actually are. The rasp of them was everywhere in our mouths. Jonathan just shrugged.

"This is usual," he said. "Sand gets into everything here."

Gets into, saturates, obliterates. Many of the town's streets appeared to be avenues of sand. They were empty, a discordant sight in a country where walking is a primary mode of transportation for most people, especially in small towns. Buildings were boarded up; trash lay everywhere. It was a postcard of desolation.

We had arranged to hire a four-wheel-drive vehicle from the NGO office. Our driver was an ethnic Kazakh man named Agytai. He stood about five feet, five inches tall, with the ruddy cheeks typical of those who spend their lives outdoors. He appeared to be in his mid-forties, but while he had been raised in the Soviet Union, his Russian evidently didn't get much of a workout anymore. Fortunately, we had with us a young local woman to fill in the gaps. (Within a year and a half, she and I would marry.) Our vehicle was a late 1990s UAZ Hunter, the Russian version of a Jeep. All six of us had to cram inside, but this wasn't unusual in Kazakhstan, even for a trip such as we were taking. The sea was eighty kilometers, or fifty miles, from Aralsk as measured directly. By road, it was one hundred bone-rattling kilometers away.

At first, near town, the road was paved, or at least had been in an indeterminate past, flanked by power lines and train tracks, the same tracks that once had carried fish from the Aral to all parts of the Soviet Union. The former sea lay to our left. It was indistinguishable from the desert to our

Village children, Kazakhstan   Photo © Kristian Ansand Walter

right. On both sides roamed shaggy two-humped Bactrian camels. In this region of Kazakhstan, they're commonly raised for their milk, wool, leather, and meat, though by tradition the local people don't eat them after Nauryz, the Central Asian New Year, which falls on or near the spring equinox. So those we saw were fattening themselves up on saltbrush, wormwood, and camel's thorn, safe until winter.

The partially paved road soon ended, giving way to a narrow two-track. We rode on the old seabed now. But while surrounded by sand, the ride was anything but soft; the underlying clay bottom had become rutted during the recent rains. We bounced so badly that our heads bumped the roof of the UAZ. The sensation was akin to cutting through choppy waves. Repeatedly, Agytai apologized for the conditions.

"This is mud," he said. "It's not my fault." But he was grinning widely. And he never slowed down.

~ ~ ~

The Aral has existed intermittently for nearly two million years, but its most familiar form dates back to the last Ice Age ten thousand years ago. From that time until the twentieth century, the sea's level did vary, and irrigation did occasionally contribute to this. But stability was the norm in recent centuries. According to Aral expert Philip Micklin, the level varied only four to four-and-a-half meters from the mid-eighteenth century to 1960. From the beginning of regular and accurate observations of the sea level in 1910 to 1960, it varied less than one meter.

Figures also vary on the sea's area at that time, but even a conservative estimate of 64,500 square kilometers (24,900 square miles) was enough to make it the world's fourth largest inland body of water, behind only the Caspian Sea, Lake Superior, and Lake Victoria. With an average salinity of 1 percent, less than a third as salty as the ocean, it was a freshwater system supporting a diverse and thriving fishery. The sea's fishing fleet caught from forty thousand to fifty thousand metric tons of fish per year, and the fish processing plants in Aralsk and Muynak were among the Soviet Union's largest. Passenger ferries full of happy Soviet tourists plied the waters between these two ports.

The sea was fed primarily by two rivers, the Amu Darya and Syr Darya, famous since antiquity for their great lengths—2,580 kilometers (1,600 miles) and 2,220 kilometers (1,380 miles), respectively. Some scholars have even identified them as two of the four rivers of Paradise. Indeed, the land between them was a sort of paradise, a wedge of life in a harsh environment that harbored a succession of civilizations over the centuries, from elegant Persian Sogdiana to colorful Arab Silk Road kingdoms, from the empires of Genghis Khan and his heirs to the emirate of Bukhara and khanates of Khiva, Kokand, and Samarkand.

Historically, the region's agriculture centered on small farmers, and the coming of the Soviets initially didn't change this much. Peasants were forced into collective farms, often violently, but at home individual families maintained a way of life as they had for centuries, raising a few cows and sheep, cultivating small fields of rice and wheat, and growing their own gardens of cabbages, tomatoes, melons, and grapes, as well as orchards of apples, apricots, cherries, nuts, and pomegranates. The region's fruit in particular was famed for its large size, rich taste, and juiciness; the hot desert sun and cool waters drawn from the Amu Darya and Syr Darya were perfect for this. Because the irrigation was done on a moderate scale, the amount of water taken was never enough to affect the Aral's level seriously. During years of drought the sea's level dropped a meter or two, but during times of heavy precipitation it rose again. Here and there was grown cotton, a plant that demands great amounts of water. Some of these cotton plantations, dating back to tsarist times, were extremely large. But as a whole, the system was more or less in balance.

Then in the 1950s, the Soviet leaders decided to expand cotton production to an industrial scale. Existing fields and huge new expanses of desert were ripped up for the "white gold." In many areas, cotton was planted right up to the windowsills of homes, displacing gardens. It pressed against the walls of nurseries and schools. Thus, anything sprayed on the cotton was sprayed on the people, even those who didn't directly work with cotton, though that number was few indeed.

The Soviets had created a new sea, a vast body of cotton, and like any sea it required an inflow of water. The largest and most easily accessible sources of this were the Amu Darya and Syr Darya. Thousands of kilometers of new canals were dug in order to irrigate an area larger than Switzerland. By 1990, it had grown to an area larger than Ireland—or approximately the Aral's original size. The new sea had finally supplanted the old one.

At first, however, there was no noticeable effect on the Aral. Water siphoned from the Amu Darya and Syr Darya was balanced by the amount of drainage water flowing back in combined with a decrease in evaporation and filtration—with less water in the rivers, there was less to lose. But more cotton was planted, more water drawn for irrigation, and new systems built that directed the drainage water to wherever was convenient, often the desert, where it completely evaporated or was lost to the sands. Thus, in about 1960, the sea began to shrink. With the exception of the small northern portion, or Little Aral, it has not stopped shrinking since. The shoreline of the larger southern portion, or Southern Aral, has retreated at least 150 kilometers (93 miles), while the average water level has dropped 22 meters, or 72 feet.

The once mighty Amu Darya and Syr Darya are but trickles of their former selves. More properly, the latter is a trickle. The former is nearly dead, exhausted along the way. In most years now, it never reaches the sea.

~ ~ ~

Listening to music on a car ride in Kazakhstan is always sure to evoke a surprise, especially if it's a long ride. Whether listening to the radio, a tape, or a CD, one is likely to hear a sometimes jarring, sometimes divinely juxtaposed mix of Russian pop, Indian film songs, Turkish dance hits, old Soviet ballads, and the occasional homegrown favorite. American tunes can remain popular in Kazakhstan for years after they've been forgotten in America. The three I heard most often in my time there were Louis Armstrong's "What a Wonderful World," Chris de Burgh's "The Lady in Red," and the live version of the Eagles' "Hotel California."

As we were too far out to pull in a radio station, Agytai played a tape, evidently his favorite tape, maybe even his only tape, for it was the only music we would hear for our entire two-and-a-half-hour ride to the sea. Typical of most compilations there, it contained a mix of hits from around the world, including George Harrison's 1987 smash "Got My Mind Set on You." I enjoyed hearing this song again after so many years. Even the second time. But after the third, fourth, and fifth times, it began sounding like a Weird Al Yankovic parody: "This song's just six words long. This song's just six words long..."

At a certain point, however, the lyrics began taking on almost prophetic connotations. Repeated like a mystic chant, they seemed to have been penned with the Aral Sea exclusively in mind, with their emphasis on "a whole lotta spending money" and "a whole lot of precious time," all in an attempt "to do it, to do it, to do it right."

As to money, a new project primarily funded by the World Bank would cost $85.8 million. By building a modern dam to keep water from draining into the Southern Aral in addition to rebuilding channels, sluices, and other waterworks along the Syr Darya, the project would thus allow the much smaller Little Aral eventually to stabilize. The philosophy behind this was that it was better to save a fraction of the sea than to lose it all. It was an important step, but it didn't address all the causes of the problem, nor would it alleviate the tragic effects. Hospitals and clinics needed to be built, staffed, and supplied, villages modernized with water treatment facilities, new roads, electricity. The bill for all this would total hundreds of millions of dollars. Kazakhstan is now perhaps in a position to begin taking up these responsibilities, but Uzbekistan flat out doesn't have the cash.

As to time, the region around the Southern Aral is by everyone's estimate locked into its current blight indefinitely. Even the region around the Little Aral could take decades to return to a measure of its former stability.

And after the expenditure of all this money and time, will the job have been done right?

II. A scam as large as the Aral disaster

If you don't plant cotton, you will be jailed.
If you don't pick cotton, you will be killed.
—Russian proverbs

These two sayings were born out of the Soviet cotton culture, Grigory Reznichenko relates in his book *Aralskaya Katastrofa* (*The Aral Catastrophe*). Both involve a play on words in the original Russian. In the first, the root word that is repeated twice, *posadit*, means both "to plant" and "to imprison." In the second proverb, the repeated root word, *ubrat*, means both "to harvest" and "to kill."

Gallows humor was perhaps the only thing that gave the region's workers any enjoyment or hope.

During harvesting season, homes, factories, schools, and universities were emptied in order to meet the demand for pickers. Some buildings remained empty for weeks until the last boll was plucked from the last thorny plant. My wife's mother, Natasha, remembers bleeding fingers from this forced conscription when she was a student, long days under a hot sun and cold nights in an inadequately supplied makeshift dormitory. The students slept on mats laid out in long rows, pressing against each other for warmth, turning as one body hourly at calls to switch sides from a succession of poor cramped figures. One season Natasha developed a bad facial twitch from frozen nerves. She ran away to home, and only a doctor's note saved her from being dragged back to the fields by the authorities. She, like the others, was never even paid the promised salary, being told that it was taken to cover her food and housing.

It was essentially state-sponsored slavery. Reznichenko, the leader of a 1988 scientific expedition to study the effects of the Aral disaster, addresses the perverse politics behind this in direct, devastating language unusual even during perestroika:

Coercion and fear drive people into the fields. Coercion and fear, but certainly not the salary. For the cotton picker, this is low indeed. And the work is exhausting and monotonous. A person must bend down ten thousand to twelve thousand times to fulfill a daily quota. To collect one hundred kilograms, for which you will be paid five rubles [about eight U.S. dollars], you must bend twenty-five thousand times. An infernal, forty-degree [Celsius] heat, poisoned earth and plants, and aridity all destroy people's health, especially that of women and children. But the more cotton there is, the happier and richer the country is![1]

Reznichenko's ironic tone makes it clear that "the country" actually meant an elite tier of well-connected officials. While the vast majority of people in the region never reaped anything but hard work and poor health from the project, those in charge made fortunes in a scam as large as the Aral disaster itself.

The scam was simple: pad the reports of cotton being produced and pocket the extra rubles. That the farmers couldn't possibly raise the harvests being reported wasn't an issue; the targets of each Five-Year Plan were unrealistic to begin with, which only encouraged more report padding. The system measured the quantity of raw cotton produced, not its quality, allowing for shortfalls to be hidden in a number of ways—understating moisture content, for example. Shortfalls at the ginning stage were covered by bribes. Bribery became rampant as more people, often relatives wanting their share, were brought in and higher-level officials bought off. Only in the early 1980s did satellite imagery of a vast area of empty fields reveal the fraud.

Due to the suicides of several key players and a flawed (perhaps purposefully so) investigation, the full scope of the scam will likely never be known, but Tsuneo Tsukatani, who has authored and co-authored a number of papers on the economics of water and land use issues in Central Asia, has reported that just between 1978 and the beginning of investigations in 1983, the Soviet state was ripped off for 4 billion rubles, or 6.7 billion U.S. dollars.

The Communist Party leader in Uzbekistan, Sharaf Rashidov, oversaw all this, but to show the extent to which such corruption is considered normal, even admired, in Central Asia, Uzbekistan's current president Islam Karimov "rehabilitated" Rashidov. A statue of him now stands in the capital of Tashkent, where a street is named after him as well. He is considered a national hero. When I lived in Shymkent, Kazakhstan, nearly every day

I passed by a ten-foot-tall statue shaped in the symbol of cotton, which, appropriately enough, was built around a water-gulping fountain. With such attitudes, it's no wonder there's little desire, political or popular, to curb the production of cotton.

Cotton is, of course, a useful—one might even say an indispensable— agricultural product whose cultivation dates back millennia. Lightweight, soft, and breathable, yet also strong, durable, and versatile, it's perfectly suited for the many goods we make of it, from archival-quality paper to our everyday clothing. But while it may be grown relatively cheaply in terms of money, it costs much more in terms of resources consumed and the effects of such consumption.

Water is the world's most important resource. Cotton demands a staggering amount—in Uzbekistan, the equivalent of nearly twenty-one thousand liters of water is needed to harvest a single kilogram of cotton, based on figures from Juliette Williams of the Environmental Justice Foundation. According to the World Wildlife Fund, a kilogram of conventionally grown cotton can require up to twenty-nine thousand liters of water to produce.

And it ranks among the world's most heavily sprayed crops. Tsukatani writes in his chapter "The Aral Sea and socio-economic development" from *Central Eurasian water crisis: Caspian, Aral, and Dead Seas,*

> For years, huge overdoses of chemical fertilizers, pesticides, and defoliants have been poured onto the cotton fields [in the Aral basin]. Among them were DDT, BHC, methyl mercaptophos, octamethyl, butifos, milbex, hexachlorane (BHO), phosphamide (dimethoate), phosalone, lenacil, ronit (Ro-Neet), yalan (molinate), sodium TCA, chlorazone, and aldrin. The chemicals are not only discharged into the rivers through drainage canals, but have also filtered through to the groundwater layer when the salinated land is flushed by huge amounts of irrigation water, thus creating capillary channels between surface water and groundwater. The capillary action carries groundwater containing minerals and chemicals to the surface, where they are left to accumulate after the evaporation of the water.

Even after DDT and butifos were banned, they were still widely used. The chemicals were applied in such heavy doses that they hung in the air in sheets, diaphanous, like mist, but which crept like fog.

~ ~ ~

"Do you smoke?" Agytai asked us several times. Two members of our group did, but they didn't want to light up in such a tight space or delay our trip by stopping. Agytai would consider this for a while, seeming nervous or agitated. Then in ten or fifteen minutes he would repeat, "Do you smoke?"

After riding for about an hour, one of our group finally asked if we could pull over for a cigarette break.

"Oh, what an excellent suggestion!" Agytai exclaimed. It was the most perfect Russian he spoke all day. He pulled over immediately and was puffing on his own cigarette hardly before the engine had died.

While the smokers indulged themselves in their pleasurable addiction, the rest of us stretched our compacted bones and gazed about the surrounding countryside. The vast plain before us not only looked like a desert, it smelled like one. Baked earth and scorching sun. Despite the recent rains, there wasn't even a whiff of sea. Like tourists, we pulled out our cameras and snapped pictures of camels. They were as obliging as cruise liners, those animals known as "ships of the desert." Who could have guessed that today they would be the only ships moving on the Aral Sea?

III. Poverty, noxious storms, and death from speeding in unstable sands

When we try to pick out anything by itself, we find it hitched to everything else in the Universe.
—John Muir

The Aral Sea issue is a classic example of the interconnectedness of the Earth's living systems, and how altering one seemingly small component can produce a tangle of large, drastic effects.

As the sea disappeared, salt levels rose, from a mild 1 percent to a choking 6 percent on average, nearly twice as salty as the ocean, killing the native fish. In the Southern Aral, where salinity is as high as 8.5 percent (and rising), only brine shrimp can survive. The loss of the fishing industry resulted in poverty and massive displacement and relocation. People in the region were not only employed as fishermen but also as sailors, mechanics, dockworkers, and workers in the fish processing plants and shipyards. Nearly all these jobs are gone. The population of Aralsk fell from eighty thousand to thirty thousand, Muynak from forty thousand to ten thousand.

The sea's moderating effect on the regional climate diminished as well. There was far less moisture evaporating into the air to condense as precipitation and smooth variations in temperature. In the 1950s, the number of rainless days a year was only 30. By 1993, it was 120, and today it's up to 150. Summers are hotter and winters colder.

Irrigation in the Aral basin has become a problem not only because it has drained the Aral's primary sources but also for a number of other reasons. The heavy doses of fertilizers, pesticides, herbicides, and defoliants used in the huge new expanses of agricultural fields (mainly cotton) eventually find their way into the drainage system that feeds the Aral, accumulating on the sea bottom. As the sea dries up, the chemicals lay exposed to the wind, which lifts them—along with salt, dust, and sand—in biblically proportioned noxious storms. Residues from these storms have been measured as far east as the Baltic Sea and as far west as the Pacific Ocean.

The bulk of noxious dust settles in the region immediately surrounding the Aral, primarily to the south and east. As much salt is now dropped on the region's cropland annually as the amount of fish once pulled from the sea. The salt seeps into the groundwater, which has become too brackish to drink. But people still do. Some have nothing else.

The region's irrigation system, much of it built on the antiquated tsarist-era system already in place, was poorly constructed to begin with, and as it aged, very little of it was repaired. Leakage and evaporation are common from these unlined, open channels. In some areas, up to 60 percent of the water drawn for irrigation is lost before it reaches the fields. In other areas, over-irrigation creates runoff, which erodes the soil, clogging both manmade and natural drainages with silt and further reducing the amount of water they can carry.

Loss of fertile soil is another catastrophe in a region that didn't have much to begin with. What is left has become salinized or, in some areas, simply buried by blowing sands. Where it had been hoped would bloom vast fields of "white gold" instead shimmer vast fields of golden desert.

Or black, red, and white desert.

A new geographic feature has been created south and east of the sea. It has been called the Aralkum (Aral Sand) or, due to its characteristic crust of toxic salt, the Akkum (White Sand). It is spreading rapidly and merging with the Karakum (Black Sand), Kyzylkum (Red Sand), and other neighboring deserts, leading some to believe the region may one day become a single desert, one of the world's largest.

At the same time that vast areas are drying up, other areas are being flooded. At the Kazakhstan-Uzbekistan border, an impromptu lake formed because the badly eroded Syr Darya could no longer carry its normal load. When Kyrgyzstan releases water from its upstream dam to generate electricity in winter, it simply spills into this new lake. Flooding due to over-irrigation and runoff is a problem in many other areas. None of this water reaches the sea.

~ ~ ~

Intimately connected with the sea are the complex river systems that feed it, in particular the delta systems of the Amu Darya and Syr Darya. Like the sea, they are dying. While this has received less attention than the disappearance of the sea itself, the loss is nearly as great, the consequences as harmful. The deltas provided the spawning grounds for many of the Aral's fish, and they were home to a profusion of other flora and fauna, including wild boars, jackals, and the Bukhara red deer, once called "the khan's flower" for its beautiful ocher coat. Livestock pastured there. People hunted, trapped, and harvested reeds for making paper and constructing homes.

The deltas also support *tugai* forests, dense communities of phreatophytes—deep-rooted plants that drink from the water table—shrubs, reeds, and other tall grasses. These communities are unique to Central Asia. There are now as little as 15 percent left. Of the 173 animal species that once lived primarily in the deltas, only approximately 20 percent survive. Of those, many, such as the Bukhara red deer, are highly endangered and literally intoxicated—stumbling in a haze of toxic salts.

The deltas no longer act as natural filters, for the dense plant communities are no longer there to retain the soil, yet another system of important natural and commercial benefit that's become a desert of deflated soils and invasive salt- and drought-resistant species.

The irony of all this is that cotton has never become the fat cash cow that many dreamed of. Corrupt officials and well-connected families have grown rich, no doubt, but the crop itself is losing ground. The cotton monoculture created a situation where diseases were able to adapt and increase. Soil fertility dropped due to nutrient depletion and erosion, while the soils became increasingly salinized.

The result? Falling cotton yields. This isn't new; they've been falling for years. Yet while the region's governments continue to praise the economic benefits of growing cotton—defiantly stating that production will not be curtailed for any reason—their people only continue to slide further into poverty. Everything they once raised on their own—animals for meat and dairy products, fruits, grains, and vegetables—they now must buy. But with cotton production falling, they have less money to purchase these staple items. Despair leads to alcoholism. My colleague Jonathan in Aralsk related that this has become so acute, some fishermen resort to drinking "spirits"—rubbing alcohol—or, when they're especially desperate, Kremlin cologne.

All this—the intense poverty, terrible water and air quality, and loss of the fishery and thus an important source of protein—has resulted in widespread malnutrition and epidemics of diseases, including anemia, cholera, dysentery, gastritis, hepatitis, jaundice, tuberculosis, typhoid fever, and various cancers. The people of Uzbekistan's Karakalpakstan region suffer the highest rate of throat cancer in the world. Their infant mortality rate is the highest in the former Soviet Union and more than fifteen times higher than in the United States. Nursing children often refuse to drink their mothers' milk because it is too saline. These circumstances have created genetic damage in the Aral basin's people, producing birth defects and leaving each new generation even more susceptible to cancer.

Perhaps most insidious of all is that biological weapons once hidden on a remote Aral island may now be accessible to anyone with the gumption to get them. *Ostrov Vozrozhdeniya* eerily translates as "Island of Rebirth" or "Renaissance Island." Indeed, the land there may again bloom—unfortunately not with the local flora, which has been decimated, but instead with weaponized plague bacteria.

From 1936 until being abandoned after the Soviet Union's dissolution in 1991, Renaissance Island saw anthrax, plague, smallpox, and half a dozen other diseases tested on a variety of animals: monkeys, donkeys, horses, rabbits, guinea pigs. Humans were also guinea pigs. In 1971, as the Aral lay dying and its ships inevitably swooned to the bottom, a smallpox outbreak triggered by a secret bioweapons field test killed dozens of people in Aralsk.

Three decades later, Renaissance Island became a peninsula linked to Uzbekistan.

Less than a year before my trip to the Aral, from May to July 2002, an American biochemical engineer with the Pentagon's Threat Reduction Agency led an expedition that reportedly cleaned up the last of the biological mess. But given how much material was deposited there in the deepest secrecy—between one hundred and two hundred tons of anthrax alone—many people aren't convinced that everything was found and destroyed.

It's said that the United States won the arms race with the Soviet Union, yet seventeen years after the latter's demise, the relics of that race remain a threat.

~ ~ ~

During our drive, we intermittently saw monuments along the roadside, simple wooden markers adorned with flowers, bright bits of clothing, and photographs.

"These people died because they were riding motorcycles and turned over," Agytai explained as if commenting on the weather.

Of all the health risks caused by the Aral's disappearance, that has to rank as the most odd: death from speeding in the unstable sands spread along the old sea bed.

We also passed three massive Muslim cemeteries set on hills that once overlooked the sea. Muslim grave markers in Kazakhstan are formed of adobe. It's the custom to show respect by enclosing these over time in domed mausoleums—the larger and more grandly decorated, the greater the respect shown. From a distance, these walled clusters of buildings looked like ancient caravan cities, only eerily devoid of bustle or any activity save that of slow decay in the sun.

The dearly departed citizens resting therein were among the more fortunate. When the region around the Little Aral was declared an ecological disaster zone, seventeen entire villages were moved, their centuries-old cemeteries abandoned, consumed by the trespassing sands.

We drove through two villages that remain, barely, Zhambyl and Tastubek. The former, once situated on a small natural harbor, was now the farther from the sea. Only fifteen families remained in the latter, providing some forty-five men to work the small fishing fleet.

If we thought that Aralsk had seemed desolate and empty, then we needed to learn a new vocabulary to describe Zhambyl and Tastubek. With their dilapidated wooden and adobe houses and streets that were nothing more than the spaces between houses, they resembled temporary nineteenth-century expeditionary outposts more than permanent settlements. Once they were among nearly two dozen fishing villages that had thrived in the Little Aral region alone. I wondered how even these two were able to keep going.

"They put some kind of fish in there," Agytai explained. "They didn't know what kind it was."

"What kind?" I persisted.

"*Kambala.*" Flounder. Here he became excited.

"The sea shrank. They put some fish in there. They didn't know what to do with it, how to catch it, but they finally figured it out."

Fishing isn't as simple as throwing out a net and pulling in whatever swims into it. Different fish live at different depths, eat different foods, and require different strategies to catch. Most are highly sensitive to changes in their environment, particularly temperature and salinity, and die if these changes are too great. That's what happened to all the Aral's twenty-four native species. Others are highly resistant to such changes, which is why flounder was introduced into the Aral. However, this new species puzzled the grizzled fishermen. It didn't behave the way they were used to fish behaving. It didn't even look right—flat, its eyes on one side of its head. No one had ever seen such a creature before. Many were revolted at the thought of eating one.

First, they learned how to catch it, and then they trained themselves to eat it. Alien-eyed or not, it was better than starving.

IV. The Aral-eaters

Everything was happening as in a fairytale: everyone did his or her own business, unaware of the result. Millions, tens of millions, of metric tons of cotton finally tipped the scales, overpowered the Aral, and the sea surrendered.

The Aral Sea died solely because of human activities and the leading role played by the Aral-eaters.

—Grigory Reznichenko

There's a serious lack of accountability in regards to the Aral that shows up in two ways. The first involves poor cooperation among the six countries linked to the Aral basin—Afghanistan, Kazakhstan, Kyrgyzstan, Tajikistan, Turkmenistan, and Uzbekistan. Each of these countries relies on water sources that, if nature were allowed to run its normal course, would ultimately feed the Aral. But negotiations for this natural resource are as winding and treacherous as the mountain waterways that provide it.

The Syr Darya begins in Tajikistan, but one of its headwaters is the Naryn River in Kyrgyzstan, where it's used to generate electricity. In summer, when demand for power is lower, the water remains dammed in a reservoir. In winter, when demand for power peaks, water is released through turbines, but this is when the downriver systems can least accept and hold water; the result is flooding, which angers Kazakhstan and Uzbekistan. Kyrgyzstan says it's simply doing what it needs to do to survive. Despite agreements to store more water in winter, it continues to disregard its commitments. In both instances, only a small portion of water reaches the Aral Sea.

The Amu Darya is formed by the conjunction of two rivers in Tajikistan, though a sizeable portion of its flow—10 percent or more—comes from Afghanistan. It then winds through Turkmenistan and Uzbekistan. All four of these countries claim their share of its waters or headwaters, and as Afghanistan stabilizes after decades of war, its draw on this resource will only increase.

Turkmenistan has made the most egregious claims, not surprising for a country whose recently deceased president-cum-dictator Saparmurat Niyazov called himself "Turkmenbashi," or "Father of All Turkmens," and grand schemes abound, some goofy, some scary. In the capital of Ashgabat, a gold statue of Niyazov slowly revolves with the course of the sun. It's forbidden for men to wear long hair and beards or for anyone to listen to car radios.

And plans call for greater irrigation of the desert to double current cotton production.

Turkmenistan's Karakum Canal is already one of the longest irrigation channels in the world. Completed in the early 1960s, it's considered the primary factor in the Aral's demise. Similar to other such works in Central Asia, half the water flowing along the leaky canal seeps into the desert, which comprises 80 percent of the country. Yet Turkmenistan not only hopes to cultivate new farms in its "virgin lands," it has also begun building a giant reservoir in its hinterlands to create a more secure water supply. Obviously, much water will soak into the thirsty sands and evaporate into the sweltering skies. Exactly how much? How will it affect Uzbekistan downstream? How will the salts and agrochemicals be removed? At what cost? If they know, Turkmen officials as of yet aren't saying. But the lake is expected to be completed by 2020, about the time the Southern Aral will be dead.

Ironically, until sixteen years ago, five of these six countries fighting for water—all but Afghanistan—were comrades together behind the Iron Curtain. Now, they share an ironclad distrust of one another.

The second way that lack of accountability regarding the Aral shows up involves failure to accept responsibility. The easiest way to do this is simply to tell the truth about why this disaster occurred. But many, particularly those who were trained in the Soviet Union, still refuse to admit, despite conclusive evidence to the contrary, that cotton irrigation is to blame.

In the summer of 2002, shortly after I had arrived in Kazakhstan, I listened to a talk in English by a Soviet-era scientist. He said that in the seventeenth century the Aral Sea didn't exist—it was nothing more than a swamp. The region's climate goes through fifty- to eighty-year cycles, and rises and declines in sea level are a natural part of these cycles. There was no evidence of livestock becoming sick yet, thus showing how reports of agrochemical pollution were wildly exaggerated. Irrigation had been going on for hundreds of years, and it had never affected the sea before. Why were people now claiming it was?

Another creative explanation for the Aral's demise (which I heard from a number of people in the region) is that an as-yet-undiscovered underground channel runs between the Aral and the Caspian seas, siphoning off water to the latter. Though no evidence has ever surfaced to support this, the textbooks my wife grew up reading proposed it as a reasonable cause.

In equally creative "solutions" to the problem, the Soviets, in typically grand thinking, considered bombing mountain glaciers in the Tian Shan and Pamirs to release their frozen waters as well as diverting the course of distant Siberian rivers via canals to replenish the Aral.

The latter was actually *seriously* considered, despite the daunting cost and complexity of the proposal and the grave environmental repercussions it would have caused. Downsizing the canal system that irrigated the cotton fields was out of the question. Strangely, modernizing these canals so that they wasted less water seemed out of the question, too. Water conservation was never included in the grand scheme to grow more cotton. To the Soviet planners' way of thinking, there was plenty of water flowing unproductively through Siberia. Why not use it? Thankfully, this plan was scrapped in 1986, though the idea occasionally resurfaces. At the request of Uzbekistan's President Karimov, Russian scientists were considering it as recently as 2004.

To accept the truth about what happened would certainly encourage more realistic solutions to the problem. Why not do so? The answer provides a fascinating glimpse into the politics of disaster. While it's outwardly fashionable to blame Soviet policies for current woes, many government institutions in Central Asia, including health and education, have remained essentially unchanged since independence. The only differences are semantic.

Thus, there's still a need to support the old Soviet line. The leaders in two of the Aral basin's countries—Kazakhstan and Uzbekistan—were prominent members of the Communist Party in their respective republics in Soviet times, as was the recently deceased president of Turkmenistan. A fourth, the leader of Tajikistan, is a former cotton farm boss.

The scientists who publicly downplay the disaster may well do so because to criticize old policies would reflect poorly on the country they were raised in and thus on themselves. In my four years of working in education in Central Asia, I sometimes encountered a similar defensive attitude, a lingering sense of "us" versus "them," as if the Cold War were still on.

It's perhaps an innate human characteristic: while we see the Aral Sea vanishing before our eyes, we're blinded by issues of greed, political and personal power, egoism, and insecurity. We become committed to our ideas just as deeply as to our self-preservation, especially those of us whose reputations rely on the acceptance of our ideas, such as politicians, academics, scientists, and writers.

To accept the truth means to accept responsibility, and few people want to do this. It's easier—and frequently more profitable—to keep throwing out the same outdated ideas, half-baked solutions, half-truths, and outright lies. When presented with conviction, these create uncertainty and confusion in the general population, which is inherently disempowering. Too often, this is exactly what those in power want.

~ ~ ~

From what I had previously read and learned firsthand on our drive, I had expected the Aral to look like a disaster area, perhaps with chemical slicks pooled on its surface. To be sure, there was at least one evident sign of disaster in the dried-up fish carcasses lining the shore. But aside from that and a few overturned rowboats and skiffs, the sea itself was unqualifiedly beautiful. Its vigorous blue waters stretched before us to the horizon. Puffy cumulus clouds hovered as if painted there, their cotton white tinted with faint suggestions of pink. Gulls wheeled overhead. We walked along the shore, picking up shells and marveling at what we had come so far to see. It was sick, we knew, very sick, but it was still alive. The sickness lay under the surface, invisible, like so many dangers in life.

In a strange way, the tranquility of the scene made it anticlimactic. I hadn't been expecting anything specific, but I'd anticipated something more dramatic. Still, I knew that we were witnessing what many citizens of Aralsk hadn't witnessed in years, some in decades.

"Older people don't go out to see the sea," Agytai explained, "and that's why they think there's no sea left."

We were witnessing what a generation in the region would perhaps never see. We could dip our hands into it, splash them about, feel the salt (and chemical) spray against our faces. As foreigners, we had the means to do so. The four of us together spent the equivalent of a local school teacher's monthly salary just to rent the UAZ. We also had the means to leave the region, to return not only to better parts of Kazakhstan but ultimately to our own homes in the United States. We had access to clean water, healthy food, and good health care whenever we wanted or needed them. We were disaster tourists, slumming it for a time to get a taste of the situation but in no danger of being consumed by it.

I felt self-conscious about this but justified my feelings with the thought that at least the money we spent to get there was going to a local organization trying to save the sea. At least the sandy bread and fruit we bought at the pitiful bazaar was helping, in a small way, the people of Aralsk. And I knew that I would write about this, about them, someday. I may have been a foreigner in the land, but I literally had my hand in the problem now. I had touched the tragedy and in doing so become part of it. Having become part of it, I had no choice but to react in some way. I wanted to be part of a solution.

Today, I'm no longer certain a realistic solution exists, not under the current political conditions. Instead, I've chosen to do the next best thing: to remember, and by writing down my memories help others to remember, not just what was done but exactly how it was done, and why, and by whom.

~ ~ ~

It's hard to believe that only fifty years ago, none of this was an issue. The Aral basin ecosystem cohered, thrived, in balance. It only took one decision—to grow cotton on an industrial scale in the desert—to wreck the balance and set the entire terrible chain of effects into motion.

Harder still to believe is that some of these effects were foreseen, but the decision was made to proceed anyway.

The Soviet planners in charge of massively expanding irrigation in the 1950s and 1960s expected the Aral Sea to dry up. Scientists had told them this would happen. The planners went ahead with their scheme for one simple reason: they determined that the economic benefits of growing cotton and other agricultural products trumped everything else that the sea could provide.

It has been reported that one Soviet official, swept up in the grand feeling of the enterprise, exclaimed, "The Aral Sea must die, just as a soldier in battle!" This is likely apocryphal, but it nevertheless aptly encapsulates a number of real factors. The planning involved was as precise as any military campaign, with specific objectives and strategies. (Indeed, the system of Five-Year Plans already in place was perfectly suited for this.) Even the name of the overarching project under which all this was mapped out was cast in military jargon: "Virgin Lands Campaign." Previously unbroken ground was to be conquered and seeded. Unlike with most Soviet propaganda, in this case there was no mistaking the language, neither its imagery nor its intended meaning. This was to be nothing short of a war on the Aral, and the Soviets laid siege to it. With supplies cut off, the Aral starved.

Those average citizens who simply hoped to earn a living and raise families became what is euphemistically termed "collateral damage." Such is inevitable in the strange economics of war. It's commonly argued that wars are economically beneficial, but to destroy a country and then build it up again is a waste of resources, both material and human. Wars may temporarily boost an economy through the production of destructive weapons, but the production of nearly everything useful is curtailed or suspended; that's why food rationing and famine are common during war.

The human costs—the numbers orphaned, widowed, crippled, maimed, emotionally scarred—are never considered, just as the Soviets never considered conservation in its war against the Aral. A comprehensive plan could have been drawn up that included the building of more efficient canals or crop rotation schedules to reduce nutrient depletion of the soil. The knowledge existed at that time. Local scientists had even invented an anti-infiltration screen that would have substantially reduced water consumption. It was never implemented.

The problem was that the authorities had no incentive—that is, no immediate economic incentive—to be bothered with conservation. They profited, and richly, from waste. The *Minvodkhoz* (Ministry of Water Management) received billions of rubles for their part in the scheme, this in a time before inflation devalued the ruble; the equivalent in U.S. dollars was also billions.

While it's easy, even comforting, to criticize the Soviets for all this, it's no different from the Ford Motor Company conducting its infamous 1970s analysis that determined it would be more cost-effective to pay off lawsuits over people killed and burned in their lethally flawed Pinto automobiles than to fix the problem. (Ford's president then, Lee Iacocca, reportedly often said, "Safety doesn't sell.") It's no different from repeated examples of companies today—from Enron to Arthur Andersen to WorldCom and on and on—that illegally manipulate their financial records in order to boost corporate bonuses and hide losses, cheating their customers and stealing from their shareholders.

By definition, all are examples of myopia, for the people involved looked at only one aspect of an issue—the bottom line—out of the myriad possible aspects to consider. They also failed to consider the consequences of their decisions.

In the case of the Aral Sea, the planners never foresaw the extreme effects of their decision: the toxic dust storms, the far-ranging desertification, the epidemics of diseases. They never calculated the financial and social costs of poverty, displacement, relocation. They either forgot about or never knew of the stockpiles of biological weapons on Renaissance Island. They had their eyes set on the economic benefits of irrigated farming, and that was all they could see. As Philip Micklin points out in *Science* magazine, "Some optimists even suggested the dried [sea] bottom would be suitable for farming."

In his groundbreaking book *After the Future: The Paradoxes of Postmodernism and Contemporary Russian Culture*, Russian essayist Mikhail Epstein writes,

> And now we can begin to define communist labor not only as the
> promiscuity of collective ownership, but also as an incestuous attitude
> toward Mother Nature. Our labor was furious and frenzied, as if we were
> possessed by insatiable desire. The all-time favorite Soviet saying became
> the maxim of agronomist Ivan Michurin: "We cannot wait for favors from
> nature; to take them from her is our task." I remember school teachers

*constantly repeating this sentence to us with a proud, ardent emphasis on
the verb "to take." Labor became a sort of rape: taking by force from Mother
Nature those favors she was not inclined to relinquish.*

What happened to the Aral wasn't "a sort of" rape. It wasn't metaphorical.
It was just as violent, and done for the same reasons of power and control.

V. After us, even flood

*And nature stepped away from us
As if we are not needed...*
—Osip Mandelstam

I've seen many strange things in my Asian travels. The Karni Mata Temple
in northern India, a holy place packed with thousands of holy rats that
scurry up, down, around, and over everything, including visitors' shoes... The
Flintstones-like cave cities in Cappadocia, Turkey, carved out of volcanic rock,
still inhabited today... The sarcophagus of the Old Testament Prophet Daniel
in Uzbekistan, a velvet-draped slab of marble eighteen meters long, for legend
says that his body continues to grow... The site I saw as the road now opened
up in front of us on the Aral's former seabed was the strangest of them all.

There they were, a fleet of ships in the desert.

There were about a dozen in all, rudders jammed into the dry mud,
anchors lowered: a redundant gesture. Two large ships, about two hundred
feet long and a thousand tons each, stood side by side so close that it was easy
to imagine sailors scurrying about to transfer fish or fuel, supplies or crew.
The smallest of the group was about one hundred feet long and one hundred
tons. It stood alone, an orphan. The others were pointed in every direction
as if heedless of their neighbors, a massive traffic jam in the making that was
stopped by the receding waters.

"It's a shame these ships were wasted," I said in English. A few minutes
later, Agytai said nearly the same thing in Russian.

He explained that as the sea retreated, the fishermen kept moving their
fleet to keep it from becoming grounded. Eventually it ended up here, the
deepest part. But this became cut off, and the fishermen could do nothing as
their ships rode the waters gently to the bottom and then rode the mud that
was left until there was no water at all, only baked earth. Through it all, the
ships remained completely upright. From a distance, a mirage shimmering
above the sand, they still appear to be at sea.

Rusting monument   Photo © Kristian Ansand Walter

"How long have they been here?" I asked Agytai.

"For a long time."

"Exactly how long?"

"A long time," he repeated. He squinted into the past and estimated it had been about thirty years, or since the early 1970s.

We parked the UAZ and walked right up to the beached relics. It was easy enough to climb on board many of them; one featured an open hatch right at ground level, though for most we had to pull ourselves over the gunwales and onto the decks. Anything useful—radios, radar, sounding devices—had been stripped long ago. Even much of the metal had been salvaged as scrap. The rest was left to rust and remember better times.

I plunged down into engine rooms that no longer smelled of diesel but of decay, scurried up ladders on masts, where I scouted not schools of fish but rather vistas of desolation. Rusting gangways gave way, imitating the roll and pitch of the sea.

Ordinarily, I'm not a rubbernecker. I don't enjoy watching disasters, either in person or on the news. For some reason, though, I was drawn in fascination to this one. Perhaps it was because it had happened long ago, enough for me to feel removed from it. Perhaps it was because these ships didn't have faces, faded eyes, or raspy, faded voices. Still, they were the ruined relics of real people's livelihoods, and I was crawling all over them as if I were a kid again. I felt a little guilty, but I was having fun. We all were. At the time, it didn't feel like exploitation, but now I'm no longer sure.

~ ~ ~

On the way back to Aralsk, our engine died. We were still some thirty kilometers from town, it was already late afternoon, and it had begun to rain. I had visions of a long, wet walk back. Fortunately, Agytai fixed the problem quickly; just as quickly, we became stuck in the sand. Even our four-wheel-drive vehicle could find no traction on the road where there was never meant to be a road. Twice we hopped out and pushed ourselves out of the mire. Eventually it stopped raining, and we found better ground.

Shortly after these incidents, we overtook a man on a bicycle, an old-fashioned model with one gear and high handlebars that forced the rider to sit up straight in his seat. The vision was so absurd that had someone told me it was a mirage I might have believed it, except that we could hear him talking to another man walking alongside him. Where they had come from, and where they were going, was an existential puzzle.

Aral Sea panorama   Photo © Kristian Ansand Walter

Though the area looked to me no different from what we had just passed through, Agytai became newly animated. He began talking about the spread of the old sea, a place where he swam and camped when he was ten, a beautiful beach with white sands.

"We had a camp there," he said, pointing to a scrubby tree. "Do you see that hill over there? That was the edge of the sea."

Though I consider myself to have a good imagination, I simply could not conjure up the image of how it once looked. The present reality was simply too glaring; it obliterated the thought of everything else. All I could see were a broad, undulating stretch of sand, a distant bluff with sand lapping at its base, and, on the horizon, three camels walking slowly through sand.

~ ~ ~

Back at the NGO office in Aralsk, hanging almost as an afterthought on a hallway wall, was a painting of the old Aral Sea. Bright blue waters with small whitecaps surged onto a beach so lovely it might have been in the Bahamas or Tahiti. A stout wooden rowboat lay parked there. Behind this, to the left, rose a steep, high bluff topped with a willow tree and thick, soft grasses. The scene was idyllic and inviting, absolutely pristine. The local woman who had come with us, my future wife, looked at it for a long moment.

"If that's what it looked like," she finally said, "then the people who ruined it are twice the jerks."

There's a Russian saying, "*Posle nas khot potop*"—"After us, even flood." It means, "If they won't affect us personally, why should we care about the consequences of our actions?" Say some teenagers enjoy a wild party in somebody's home while the parents are away. When the parents return, those responsible for the destruction will be long gone. *Posle nas khot potop.*

The Soviets had their party. The rest of the world is now aware of all that happened, but there's not much to do about it; the liquor cabinet was raided, the good china broken, and the partygoers dispersed as soon as they heard footsteps on the staircase. We simply have to roll up our sleeves and put our house in order.

VI. Our Aral seas

Whiskey's for drinking; water's for fighting over.
—American folk saying

It's easy for us to feel that the folly of a poorly thought-out and constructed irrigation system and the resulting waste is something that could only happen "over there," clear proof of failed Soviet ways, and not here in America. In the same way that many Soviet-era scientists and other professionals still feed us their Cold War propaganda, it's clear that many Americans feel our system is inherently superior across the board, at all levels.

Yet scarily, many of our practices are every bit as wasteful as those unlined, open canals in Central Asia.

Even in the arid regions that I've lived in, such as southern Idaho and eastern Washington, which average less than twelve inches of precipitation per year, it's common to witness people watering their emerald lawns during the hottest part of a summer's day. Golf courses stand out as lush oases. Houses proliferate in dry brown foothills, fed by municipal water systems that draw from rivers never meant to spread their reach so far.

Why are we so wasteful? It's as easy to buy a drip irrigation system, which allows water to soak into the ground, as it is to buy a spray system. It's as easy to set a timer to water in the morning and evening, when evaporation is much slower, as it is to set it for the hottest part of the day. Turning off the faucet while brushing one's teeth is easy, saving on average five gallons of water per minute. Installing low-flush toilets and low-flow showerheads pays for itself many times over. Given how Americans love convenience and thrift, it would seem that we would naturally embrace such conservation, which takes little or no effort beyond fitting it in our normal routines and saves us resources and thus money.

But conservation isn't about effort or cost. It's about changing habits. And when confronted with this, people often become defensive. Americans in particular don't like to be told what to do. Only when faced with an emergency do we take the necessary steps to meet it.

We have an emergency.

America has its own Aral Sea. It's called the Ogallala Aquifer.

Based on scale and the number of people that potentially could be affected, the situation with the Ogallala is actually worse. It underlies approximately two hundred thousand square miles of land, thus covering an area eight times as large as the Aral once did. The aquifer is a major source of fresh water for the arid Great Plains region, a source tapped by eight states: Colorado, Kansas, Nebraska, New Mexico, Oklahoma, South Dakota, Texas, and Wyoming. A third of all corn grown in the United States is irrigated with water from the Ogallala, and our great "cotton bowl" draws from it as well. It's the largest underground water system in the world. It's also one of the fastest disappearing.

How much water is left varies, depending on the section of the aquifer one talks about. In some sections, the water table is dropping three to five feet per year. Some estimates say the entire aquifer may be depleted in only twenty to thirty years. Even the optimists don't give it more than a century if current conditions persist. Either way, there are children being born in the region today who, if they ultimately don't move away as many already have, will likely see their taps run dry, permanently. As with the Aral, the primary reason for the aquifer's disappearance is over-pumping water for irrigation.

There are other parallels. When we hear of how the Soviets considered diverting Siberian rivers thousands of kilometers away to feed the Aral, it sounds like the scheme of some Dr. Strangelove character. Yet we have our own schemes just as grandiose—and potentially catastrophic. Many of these involve building pipelines from the Great Lakes to any number of water-starved regions in our country. More than thirty-three million people, or approximately 10 percent of the combined populations of the United States and Canada, live in the Great Lakes basin and rely on its waters. To pipe water out of this basin would put this huge number of people at risk of serious water shortages. The Great Lakes hold approximately 21 percent of the world's surface freshwater and a staggering 84 percent of North America's, yet they recharge at the rate of only 1 percent per year. This is primarily due to their small watershed; while they cover an enormous amount of land, they drain a relatively small portion. Should they begin shrinking, less evaporation would result in a drier surrounding climate, decreasing rainfall and thus decreasing another source of the lakes' recharge, exacerbating the problem.

This would be exactly what happened to the Aral Sea. Yet while the majority of scientists are adamantly against any pipeline plans, the idea is often bandied about by politicians and others as a solution to water problems in other parts of the United States, mostly the desert West. Demands for water are particularly high in our most populous state, California, where a number of lakes have disappeared or are disappearing.

One of the most famous examples is Owens Lake. It was drained within a period of twenty years in the early part of the twentieth century when the City of Los Angeles—led by a corrupt mayor and a cadre of ruthless businessmen using deceit and bribery—diverted water from the Owens Valley, a story that in part inspired the 1974 film *Chinatown*. But the lake is far from being a historical footnote. Today, dust containing toxic elements such as arsenic and cadmium is blown from the dry lakebed in fierce storms throughout the valley and beyond. It's the largest point source of particle pollution in the country. The only viable solution was to flood the lakebed shallowly and plant native salt grasses to keep the dust down, which cost more than four hundred million dollars to set up and requires more than twenty million dollars a year in water to maintain.

Then there's the Salton Sea. In the past decade, millions of fish have died due to the increasing salinity of its waters as the lake level falls; they could all be dead, every fingerling and egg, by the time the Southern Aral completely disappears. The Salton's story is the same, only in this case San Diego is to blame for sucking the source waters away. Some people feel this sea isn't worth saving. After all, its current form dates to only a century ago, when a canal breeched and sent the Colorado River spilling into the Salton Sink. But should the Salton dry up, it will result in dust storms full of pesticides, salts, and heavy metals, as at Owens Lake, only the exposed area would be more than three times larger.

The projected reclamation cost? Up to one billion dollars, and that to save but a portion of the sea.

Like the Soviets, we justify our environmentally destructive decisions in the name of economics. But when faced with the price of cleanup, which often runs into the hundreds of millions of dollars, it becomes clear that even economically our decisions are unsound. Ultimately, we pay. The issue is really over who profits in the short term. Environmental destruction is systemic, part of our way of life and doing business, but it's a system that benefits a relatively few wealthy people at the expense of the vast majority. It's devilishly clever in how it moves money around. The public pays in several ways. We pay in taxes that subsidize many companies or in the loss of tax income when these companies are given special incentives. We pay for their products. We pay in absorbing the ill effects of their production. Finally, we pay for the cleanup.

~ ~ ~

At the time of the writing of this essay, gasoline prices are dominating the news headlines, yet no one seems to think anything of paying $1.69 for a liter of bottled water—not Perrier, not even generic mineral water, but just plain, filtered water in a bottle. Often it's simply municipal tap water in pretty packaging. Yet that price translates to an astounding $6.40 a gallon, more than double the price of gas. In some markets, bottled water sells for up to $10 a gallon.

According to a 2006 study published by the Earth Policy Institute, "The United States is the world's leading consumer of bottled water, with

Americans drinking 26 billion liters in 2004." This even though "in the industrial world bottled water is often no healthier than tap water, [and] it can cost up to 10,000 times more." When did it happen that a resource that constitutes 70 percent of our bodies, that we die from lack of after only seven days, that surrounds us in oceans, lakes, rivers, glaciers, clouds, and the living tissue of every living thing, became such an expensive commodity?

It's analogous to the situation in the Aral Sea region. The people there were told to grow cotton, and they came to rely on the cash from that crop to pay for basic food necessities they once grew themselves for a fraction of the cost. We, too, have done exactly what we were told to do—build our factories, log our forests, mine our mountains, and irrigate our farms—and we came to rely on the cash from these activities to buy the very resource we once enjoyed for free, before our activities polluted it and made it scarcer.

Everywhere on the planet, it's the same. The United Nations estimates that 1.1 billion people—one-sixth of the world's population—have unsafe drinking water supplies. The 2003 UNESCO report "Water for People, Water for Life" states that by 2050, a minimum of 2 billion people will live in countries severely lacking freshwater. The figures could run as high as 7 billion people. As French President Jacques Chirac suggested at the 2003 World Water Forum, this century could be a time of "tension and water wars." Or to use the old American folk saying, "Whiskey's for drinking; water's for fighting over."

The BBC has identified twelve water "hot spots." These include the Aral Sea and the Ogallala Aquifer. Two hot spots, Israel and Iraq, are ravaged by war. Others are in countries with tremendously high, dense urban populations, such as Mexico, India, and China, exemplifying how it's impossible to talk about water shortages—or environmental pressures of any kind—without talking about the exploding human population and unsustainable economic development.

In China, already more than 300 million people—or more than the entire population of the United States—live in rural regions that lack potable water. In a country that's more than a quarter desert, with as little as 7 percent of the planet's fresh water but 20 percent of the population, this problem is certain to grow worse.

Their answer? Work has already begun on a massive diversion project to bring water thousands of kilometers from the monsoon-soaked south to Beijing and other dry northern cities. It's the largest such project ever undertaken.

Ship graveyard   Photo © Kristian Ansand Walter

VII. Recent gains—or are they?

In every drop of water, there is a grain of gold.
—Uzbek proverb

The $85.8 million joint Kazakhstan-World Bank project to revive the Northern Aral Sea is showing results well ahead of schedule. A new dam prevents water from draining into the Southern Aral, while improved waterworks along the Syr Darya allow more water to flow into the Northern Aral. This resulted in the water level rising three meters within seven months, well ahead of the five to ten years experts had expected. Already nearly a thousand square kilometers of dried seabed have been reclaimed, and the region's climate is changing. Clouds are coming back, as are the rains. Fish— and not just salt-resistant flounder but also pike, carp, and bream among more than a dozen species—are being caught again, though the waters still don't reach the old ports; the fishermen must drive every morning to the sea. But it's closer. Old villagers who thought they would never see the sea again now weep at the prospect of doing so. The outmigration of people from the region has slowed considerably, and some have even returned. The standard of living is slowly rising.

It's all so encouraging that the government of Kazakhstan has negotiated with the World Bank for another loan, this one for $126 million, to build a second dam that's hoped will bring water back to the long-abandoned former port of Heralsk. Associated works with this project may even transform Aralsk into a port again.

There has been much congratulatory talk about this, as there should be. But the Northern Aral is also called the Little Aral for a reason. Too often overlooked is that the Southern Aral—the much larger portion, and the portion suffering most severely—is doomed to be lost to evaporation. This oversight has led to some pronouncements that would be humorous if they didn't ultimately reveal the continuing effects of the disaster and the underlying biases that shape judgments and analyses of it.

"World Bank restores Aral Sea" boldly proclaims the headline to an article by Christopher Pala in *The Washington Times* dated April 1, 2006. The timing of publication was fitting, for the headline was highly deceiving. The article actually referred to the project expected to revive the Little Aral, not the entire sea.

The Little Aral represents but a fraction of the Aral's former size, and only two-thirds of this smaller sea is expected to be saved, provided that Kazakhstan follows through properly on the second phase of its collaboration with the World Bank. A projection made at the beginning of the first phase estimated that the Little Aral would stabilize at 3,500 square kilometers (1,350 square miles), or little more than 5 percent of the Aral's total former size. Yet Pala enthuses, "It would achieve one of biggest reversals of an environmental disaster in history." He appears to have overlooked 95 percent of the sea when he wrote that.

While saving the Little Aral is a desirable goal, one worth the effort, it's difficult to understand how saving 5 percent of something can deserve any more than muted enthusiasm. Aralsk may once again enjoy some measure of its old prosperity, but Muynak, the former fishing port in Uzbekistan that once rivaled Aralsk, will never be revived. And no one is claiming that the noxious dust storms will entirely cease, that the region's climate will fully be restored, or that the health problems of its people will dramatically improve overnight.

The headline, with its focus on the World Bank, also shows our persistent bias that any problem can be solved as long as we throw enough money at it. Even more revealing, it suggests that the World Bank alone is responsible for whatever gains have been made regarding the Little Aral. The Kazakhstani people, who have been gamely dealing with the mess for decades, are relegated to the role of bit players.

Another article by Pala in the *International Herald Tribune* reveals another persistent belief, one almost religious in nature: that of technology as savior. In that article, Russian Aral Sea specialist Nikolai Aladin is quoted as rejoicing, "What man has destroyed, man can now restore."

Superficially, this sounds poetic, hopeful, even life-affirming, a statement of humanity's desire to do more good than harm. Looked at more deeply, it reveals one of our greatest troubles: poor moral development paired with a science-fiction perception of science.

There's nothing inherently bad about science. Neither is there anything inherently good. It's simply a tool. To be used effectively, it must be matched with good judgment. This would seem to be so obvious as to be commonsensical. Yet repeatedly, all over the world, we plunge ahead with our technological plans even when those plans have grave flaws, because we believe that time will ultimately produce better technology to fix those flaws. For example, given the half-life of radioactive isotopes, all current nuclear waste containment sites are temporary, but we continue to bury nuclear waste in the belief that we will build better containment sites. Someday.

This uncritical belief that our science and technology can fix anything is arrogant, and to call it anything less is to fail to accept responsibility for our actions. Rather than working continually in crisis mode to fix our problems, we should learn how to avoid making those problems in the first place.

For the most part, however, we have gone about our business as usual and worried about the consequences later. This is an immature and irresponsible attitude. As adults, we should understand the value of review and the wisdom of planning—the subtle back-and-forth of learning from the past and looking into the future that keeps us properly focused on the present. Yet we continue to abuse the environment and then scramble madly to soothe it, all the while castigating ourselves for knowing better, the behavior of addicts or fetishists. We flagellate ourselves to atone for our sins and then say that we deserved it. We're masochists, and I don't use this word lightly. Gratifying ourselves with short-term economic pleasure and self-congratulatory technological boasts at the cost of long-term devastation and pain is nothing short of masochism.

Our behavior toward the Earth can properly be called sadistic. We think little of harming it because it appears to be inert and thus immune to harm, a ball of dust that only through our prodding intervention can be coaxed into providing what we desire. Yet it's our home as surely as any four walls that shelter us.

As we have diligently sought to understand the Aral's disappearance, so we must also diligently seek to understand our behavior. These are linked as intimately as hydrogen and oxygen in every molecule of water. But while much emphasis has been put on what it might take to save the Aral—more money, better dam projects, improved irrigation technologies—I've only read hints of the most fundamental part of the solution: a complete change in our attitude toward nature.

~ ~ ~

Some decisions in life are small, such as deciding to hit the snooze button and sleep for five more minutes. Some are large, such as choosing whom to marry. All have consequences, and these consequences require us to make more decisions, leading to an interlinked chain of events that can appear to be the will of fate. There are those who would argue that economic and political circumstances determine our decisions, that the pressures Soviet planners faced were too great for them to act according to their consciences. Even if true, it doesn't negate the decisions. Economic conditions and political pressures are not causes for morally unsound actions. They are factors. As such, they need to be considered, but not at the expense of considering the full range of factors that shape an issue.

In my reading for this essay, I encountered streams of facts and statistics—a flow that if it were water might save the Aral. These are important to know, and I've gathered many of them here. However, no matter how assiduously this information was researched and presented, and no matter how damning it may be, it conspicuously stands in absence of any direct condemnations of the scientists, planners, and politicians for the weak moral foundation that gave rise to their actions.

Facts and statistics are only ways of reckoning the *effects* of the disaster, not its causes. Admittedly, the causes in many ways cannot be reckoned, because they directly relate to our human nature, which inherently cannot be enumerated. Because it's so complex and resists enumeration might explain why so few scientists and writers have been willing to explore it. Grigory Reznichenko hinted at it when describing the difficulties he experienced in finding a publisher for his book: "Party leaders in Russia and the Central Asian republics were and are sickened by glasnost, even though they introduced it, for it reveals the unseemly actions of the powers that be, their plundering attitude toward nature, the barbaric destruction of its resources." I will be more direct: these men (and the principal players were all men) lacked even the moderate sense of moral values that could have prevented the disaster. They lacked integrity.

According to *Merriam-Webster's Unabridged Dictionary*, one of the definitions of integrity is "avoidance of deception, expediency, artificiality, or shallowness of any kind." The last element in that list reads like a bad pun, but there's no doubt that had the Soviet planners possessed integrity, they could have avoided the shallowness of today's Aral Sea.

Anyone who uses words such as "integrity" runs the risk of moralizing, or at least of being accused of moralizing, but there's much greater risk in not facing such issues honestly. Moreover, it would be cowardly. It's not easy to develop a sense of responsibility and act on it. But we have seen ad nauseum—literally, to the point of physical sickness—the results of people taking the easy way.

~ ~ ~

Would the Aral have dried up on its own again someday? Likely, yes—in a few thousand years. But humans have catastrophically sped up the process; mapmakers can hardly keep up with the changes. The local flora and fauna have had no time to adjust, perhaps to adapt or migrate to other areas.

Nor have the local people.

Activities that lack balance reflect the unbalanced nature of those performing them. That we prize economic benefits above all others is unbalanced. That we seek short-term over long-term gains is unbalanced. That we put our full faith in technology rather than in natural systems is unbalanced. This is not indicative of a healthy species. Earning an adequate income is necessary, to be sure, but maintaining strong family and community ties and a respectful relationship with our surroundings is equally important and costs nothing. To use technology consciously and conscientiously can be useful, but to continue willfully pursuing activities that are unsustainable reflects a deep-seated aggression not only against the environment but also against ourselves. *When we try to pick out anything by itself, we find it hitched to everything else in the Universe.*

Humans have been engineering the environment for millennia, and we will continue to do so. Many, including me, would argue that this is as natural as any act any creature makes in this world. But to what *degree* do we have a right to do this? Do economic needs justify actions that help to feed and clothe us even as they destroy the environment? Do we take priority over all other living things?

There must be limits. Difficult circumstances don't absolve us from our moral responsibilities, from taking a long-term, balanced view in which human interests are weighed equally with the interests of other animals and the plants, water, and air they need to survive. In the end, we need these to survive as well, as the Aral disaster makes painfully clear.

VIII. Conclusion

Nothing is farther away than yesterday; nothing is closer than tomorrow.
—Kazakh proverb

Many of those writing about the Aral Sea lament the massive amounts of chemicals blown from the dry seabed, but precious few lament that these chemicals were used in the first place. Others are troubled that the stockpiles of biological weapons on Renaissance Island may fall into the wrong hands, but I've encountered none who seem troubled that these weapons were made or who even question their need. Apparently, it's a given for most scientists and journalists that agriculture and synthetic chemicals go together as naturally as air and water, that bioweapons are to humans as babies to their mothers. We rarely question these assumptions in the name of "being realistic," but nothing will change until we choose to face the contradictions in what we've been trained to believe.

The large-scale industrial model of farming isn't inherently more viable than traditional or progressive methods, not in all circumstances. Yet

Cargo of birds   Photo © Kristian Ansand Walter

Americans are told that we need the agribusiness model in order to be more productive, even though we're already so productive that we grow more food than we can eat or export, and the government pays farmers subsidies *not* to grow more food.

The creation of inhuman tools of butchery doesn't arise out of inevitable need. A biological weapon can never feed, house, or clothe us, can never offer us condolence, wisdom, or hope. It has one purpose: to kill in a widespread, efficient, and psychologically terrifying way. Yet when these weapons are accidentally released into the environment or tested on humans—as they inevitably are—we're repeatedly surprised at the results. We're concerned about the bioweapons on Renaissance Island only because we fear that terrorists might find and use them; we expect large industrialized countries to manufacture such weapons. We're told that they provide security. But can we truly maintain security with them if we must constantly worry about that security being breached?

We're living in an age when doublespeak is threatening the integrity of our language as never before, and this threatens the integrity of our very selves. As surely as we shape language, so does language shape us. We cannot make statements such as "science has not determined the cause of global warming" without feeling its ambivalence, becoming the confusion itself, even as polar ice caps melt and temperatures continue rising. We cannot praise the economic benefits of ecologically devastating practices without coming to believe our own words that indeed the greatest profits provide us with the greatest benefits, even as other benefits such as clean water, clean air, fertile soils, and healthy communities disappear, unenumerated, before our eyes. Without understanding that what we say and believe is connected to what we do, consequences tend to look like cruel accidents, twists of fate, the whims of God. They are not.

The Aral Sea disaster wasn't inevitable, nor are the current crises that loom before us: the falling Ogallala Aquifer, our disappearing lakes, or even global warming. Worldwide water wars are not inevitable. They may easily be avoided by restructuring the way we interact with our environment, with our neighbors, and with ourselves. This is not as grand or difficult as it might sound. Conservation is not a new idea. Neither is cooperation between nations. We have all the tools we need. Human ingenuity and creativity are boundless. If we took a fraction of the energy that we currently use to create weapons and fight wars and instead invested it in constructive projects— building water purification and desalination plants, improving existing waste water treatment and sanitation systems—we would go a long way toward ensuring a clean supply of water for all, with plenty of profit to keep everyone happy.

We must begin to calculate the true cost of our actions. This requires thinking much more broadly and long-term than we currently do. It also involves asking tough questions. They are tough not because they are complex but rather because they are broad, and addressing them requires broad consensus, coordination, and cooperation among all the many elements of society—the hardest kind of work, but the most essential in any democracy:

Why are we not more mindful of conserving water? Of conserving all our natural resources? Can we in good conscience continue to buy cotton or any other products from countries that engage in socially exploitive and environmentally destructive practices? Shouldn't we use our economic influence to foster positive change? Shouldn't we change our own destructive practices, now, while it's relatively less painful, before they bloom into crises? Why put off doing what we ultimately must do?

We have a choice.

The Technicolor mural in the train station in Aralsk could be a blueprint: of how humans can cooperate to help each other when the call is made.

Or the image of ships riding the sands could, if we're not careful, end up representing more than poor Soviet planning and a disaster in a relatively sparsely populated region of the world. It could become a metaphor for our own lives. ◾

ENDNOTE

[1]*The Aral Catastrophe* is written in Russian. This and subsequent passages from it, as well as all other phrases in Russian, were translated by my wife Valentina Fearnside and myself.

Midwesterner

Anthony Opal

The sound of a thin metal shovel
scraping the concrete.

The pale blue of early morning.
A piece of the moon

still visible
like a water-stain on the sky.

And I am a Midwesterner, I think.
As a single car aches

by emitting
white clouds that tumble and dissipate.

And then the silence.
The insulation.

The nearly imperceptible cracking
of snow and ice.

The Sky Holds Darkness

Anthony Opal

The sky holds darkness
just as the soil holds light.

What is meant by this

can be found inside a fig:
the bruised name of God,

the coppery seeds reoccurring.

Do you remember the way
Saint Francis shyly

named the owls that night?

How you turned to me,
all lamplit and flickering,

the blackened core of dusk

turned inside-out, the beating
heart of Christ

suddenly bare

across your face,
and then the beginnings of rain.

The One Who Gets Away
Nikki Zielinski

Sooner or later, it will be you
who falls like a cardinal's red feather
into the burning Cuyahoga

to be pulled from the oiled rapids
to the shocking, clear water
where the Chagrin River waits.

And whether you drift east
or whether you drift west,
you will forever find yourself

a thumbprint on the window
of some prettier city. Because you are
taken. Because you belong

to the city that seethes and smokes and sends
the screech and clatter of steel mill
like a serenade into the night. The city

that is never not lit fluorescent
that is never not thickly sweating.
The city that carries its workers home

blackened with oil and ash, so spent
they fail to make it to the bath
before falling exhausted into bed

so that the sheets of all the city are stained
and the smell soaks into the bricks
and the pews and the broken glass

and the boards that read *Condemned*
and hang over doors of houses
that appear to be empty

but behind which lingers
the sound of something scraping.
And so what.

Out where the train tracks still run,
a jagged hole in the chainlink
is the entrance to the shell

of a burned-down textile mill,
its floor a swirl of melted plastic buttons.
There, in the ash, in the dirt, in the remains,

you once lay, like so many other girls,
and though the buttons bit into your back,
never once wanted silk sheets.

Emzara, After the Flood
Nikki Zielinski

Everything now is water—sheen on slick deck,
damp flap of sail's canvas, apples rotten in a rotting bowl.
Two spiders weave in the corner. Termites chew nests
in the walls. You sweat against me and say nothing.

I can't sleep. I am trying to remember their names—
the ragged old woman who wandered the market,
unsteady hands swiping coins from our pockets.
Our neighbors who moaned a-twist in the weeds
while their daughter stole slop from the livestock.
And that drunken delinquent—what was his name?—
who spent hours at our door, smearing mud on the walls
and offering to clean them for a price . . .

Tell me now, Noah, if I may speak: Were we brave
to save just what was worthy of love? The silk black panther,
the shell grey dove, but not the bruised glutton who wept
over his figs? To rescue black widows, gloss-backed and poisonous—
the vipers hissing venom—but leave the adulteress
who turned her sweating back toward heaven
and moaned until the water took her lungs?

Maybe, husband, this is justice: Each night I lie
bound to your side in these damp sheets and wish
that you'd left me behind, for the clean, simple crush
of all that water, quick, on my chest. It will be eternity
before your sweat wrests the breath from my body.

Underwater

Peter F. Murphy

It's not the water, it's the air that makes traps
rust. In the river they'd be fine. The minute
they break the surface, they start to rot.

Jimmy tipped the twenty-horse Merc
over the transom almost following
it in. Precautions poured out with the smell
of stale beer from closing-time. Four years
on the Pacific taught him the bob-and-weave
that gave dance steps to his lurch.

We traced his line all morning in hope
of a beaver to nail round for a coat,
or a mink we'd stretch long and skinny
on a board rubbed smooth. Bounty to cover
bar tabs and calm alimony's rage. Muskrat
saddles fried with chicken gizzards
would be payment enough.

Jimmy pulled the curved spring over blunt
jaws past a trigger filed thin. With bare hands
he cracked black ice and placed traps in runs
among the weeds. His fingers half-frozen,
he never tripped a pan.

The stiff wire holds their head back
so they can't chew off a leg.

Say Water & Memory
Randall Horton

the color of memory is a very slight
blue hue.

I.

       & say you can't see it
millions of molecules
               wrapped round
dna   skin & bone
   solvent over time over decades
innocently rain falls into an ocean
   comingling with history's echo...

2.

       & say she swam out to the first wave
shuddering & did not know why
    later staring at protons
nuclei   she never tried to recreate
her busy silhouette against time...

3.

       & say she has never moaned
  the spilled cry of water
             in block letters
the angled pain not revealed
made no sense   in the revision
people cannot live without water
          the way it slaps
back into furious moments...

4.

      & say 30,000 feet above the atlantic
will not save you
      you must plunge
deep   down below white caps
rushing up from the bottom
there is a story to recapitulate...

5.

      & say stories are hidden
in puka shells
tiny prayers bombed
      into fragments the incantation
hovering a halo around a sinner...

6.

faith evaporating   unstrung puppets
headless through pitch dark anarchy

The District's Park
Randall Horton

against the grain her arm
    mingles around mine softly
                i feel
oppositional current thick her blood
    a future blueprint of children
          we have
none   so eclectic the goldenrod
    sky   littered with mallards quivering
two clicks starboard
                   the wind—:
swirls respond in ripples
    the lake's fabric holds (us)
             be-
tween night & day is it love
    i ask to not know   how
           high
a function of time am i sprung
    into her magic i need to
          swan dive-
fade away honey she jazzes
as if music interrupted
    behind her milk crates i go
          natal
right then infected my hips
motionless the body still
          listening
for breakdown—: i jump in the riddle
       to solve her paradox
constantly shifting my nose
    an illusion i smell wide open.

When They Cross the Bridge
Randall Horton

just above whitecaps a colony
the grammar of forgotten bodies

overflowing between bars male
populous bright with melanin faces

brown always relative to law
of profiling perhaps racial equates

just above whitecaps a colony
a mural of displaced residents

line the walk to chow in prison
across river water collect calls

begin with regret begin with banjo
twang & pluck of voice & twang

time will move ahead no one will
visit from the district no one will

remember youngin' in cell block b
digging in shoebox for metal-

spoon he once shoved a blade deep
years flowed from a gray-haired judge

what remains is alpha-omega
momma's boy stitches moth wings

dreaming he will drift into golden
above whitecaps until no more.

Dear Etheridge Knight
Randall Horton

bizarre blue-green mallards climbing methodically
over & through the point. a silver kayak slices
a chilled river, further out to the granite sculpture,
cherry blossoms have not come into bud. the hull
of the kayak glides across aphotic water smoothly
the district will sleep tonight. angles of ocher contort
random images, no one sees simple erasures
inerasably a little boy dancing by the wharf,
a pool of memory circles him spinning like bracelets,
one by one minutes fall into reverie, arriving midday
the sun is furious. dear etheridge tell me how
do i enjoy innate wonders between space & time?
do you know i am leftover fragments sprawled
above rolling green grass looking up at the zenith
float away? i have been reduced to sound, unseen
motion of alphabets. poor lulu will not be
the heroine, will not be rescued. a jungle out there
anxious with no eyes, no beat to feel love, now
i am sisyphus running uphill to brave the eddy
in darkness, to catch hope, childhood innocence.

It Used to Be Called Casino Magic
Ellen Ann Fentress

THE HOLLYWOOD CASINO suggests 1920s California, while its landscape suggests, well, trees. The driveway is lined with just-purchased palms, hurried into place with six-inch stubble on top instead of regulation fronds. From the Hollywood Casino's perch at the end of felt-green grounds, entering cars miss the fact that the seventeen-day-old casino is a new planting, too. It is a replacement built in front of the corpse of the old casino, annihilated by Katrina twelve months ago. All that remains of the old casino is a gray shredded mass floating behind it. It used to be called Casino Magic.

Mississippi casinos use air filtration to take care of cigarette smoke, and a window-free design to take care of the rest of the world, which runs on clocks and notions of responsibility. Even that unending blip blip blip of an acre of slots does its part. It sounds like a giant whirring demonstration of matter itself, a model of string theory's eternal pulse. Casino connoisseurs see slots as a pretty basic life form as well, the no-skills haunt of gambling grannies. The front of the casino is for the hapless. Real players have the sense to go upstairs to the Poker Salon, where know-how improves a gambler's odds. It's where Marie Cox deals their cards.

~ ~ ~

She works 9 to 5, same as a banker. Marie, with a long brown ponytail and round wire-rimmed glasses, dresses in casino camo: black pants and long-sleeved black collarless shirt. Casino uniforms blend in for the same reason casinos are windowless, which is the same reason grocery stores keep the bread and the milk in back. Customers need pulling in, whether the chips are the white cardboard kind at the Hollywood Casino or Ruffles at Kroger. To that end, dealers are almost invisible, unembodied agents of hospitality keeping the customers on track. The day is cerulean blue outside, but inside is a clockless realm with Annie Lennox throbbing, "Sweet dreams are made of this. Who am I to disagree?" over the sound system. Ten players at a time circle Marie's oval green-felt table. Its padded rim has built-in drink holders. At the table, a lady orders Kahluas and cream and flirts with the craggy-faced senior next to her. To Marie's right, a twenty-one-year old in tattoos and denim has a cold Bud and lukewarm luck.

At the end of her shift, Marie emerges into the yellow sun in the parking lot. She turns left at the exit. On U.S. 90, she is in the thick of what is called "the new normal:" the hollow Exxon remnant, the new Wendy's, the new Lowe's that glows with its fresh white paint and profits. Next to the Lowe's lot, Four Seasons Palms has set up, in hopes that recovering customers will buy one of their burlap-wrapped palms along with their Lowe's paint and lumber.

Marie's commute takes twenty miles extra since the Bay St. Louis bridge is gone, a problem of nineteen thousand drivers each day. Looping back and forth to use undamaged I-10 bridges to drive anywhere is not the only complication in going home. The chief complication is she has no home, not since Katrina. She still can't believe it, nor does the collection agency, which writes her snippy letter to say that it just might repossess the house, gone for a year now, if she doesn't resume the monthly payments. Marie is giving the agency no choice, the letters point out.

Marie turns north at the Menge Avenue exit and winds through inland Harrison County, where posters advertising DNA home paternity tests are nailed to the roadside pine trees. This is the territory of $300,000 homes on treeless plots, rotting shacks and the occasional corrugated steel church. Marie turns on to dirt tracks and bumps up to the white trailer. The garden patch in front of the trailer is at its September zenith with sunflowers, tomatoes and watermelons. The front steps cut through the middle. From inside, she can hear her husband Joe is watching the Weather Channel.

"Hey."

"How was it?" asks Joe, sitting in the new blue and cream plaid chair. He wears shorts, flip flops and his regular cheerful humor. His silver hair and his white T-shirt—it stretches over his middle—make his sunburned face look even redder.

"It was OK." She tells herself not to ask him. She does anyway. "Did we get anything from FEMA today?"

"No." His round face stiffens. The trailer's atmosphere tenses. He changes the subject brightly. "The Braves are on tonight."

Marie keeps a basket of Hostess cupcakes on the counter. She picks one up and pulls the cellophane wrapper apart. She finds her saucer in the drainer, where she left it this morning. It is almost the only thing left from her house. Her neighbor found it a few days after the storm, upside down under an inch of debris in her yard. It feels cool in her palm. A saucer is almost something you can cuddle. She is grateful for that, she guesses. She cradles it most of the time she's at home, inventing ways to use it—for a sandwich or her coffee cup. She centers her cupcake in the indention where the coffee cup should go. She got the saucer as a wedding present in April 1970. The pattern's name is Springdale, and it sat stacked away for thirty-five years of marriage. This and a few poker chips—she collects them from all the casinos—are the only things she found back on Trautman Avenue. She thinks back on all her possessions like lost children she longs to touch one more time. Why didn't she appreciate everything? It's not that she's materialistic. She likes things simple. She dresses in shorts and skips makeup. Her social life is watching Monday night football at her daughter's or grilling at her brother's.

Yet things define us, the basic and familiar most of all. That's what she misses, her framework: the photos, the dining room set that was Joe's mother's, her two lemon trees close enough to the back deck to lean out and pick their lemons. She reaches for another cupcake. She's smoking again and buys her Hostess cupcakes by the box. These cupcakes are devil's food, the kind with chocolate icing and rhythmical loops of white icing on top, like so many I-10 detours back to a trailer that's not even home.

"I wish I could see it like God." If there were a cosmic security camera, Marie wants to see the tape of what happened at 651 Trautman Avenue in Long Beach, Mississippi, on the morning of August 29, 2005. Her unanswered questions gnaw at her. It's the same unfinished dynamic of an Army family's wanting all the details of a child's death in Iraq. Marie wonders what it looks like when the tidal surge hit the south side of her house. She wishes she could see how the walls cracked, and at what wind velocity her roof ripped open. She wonders what it looked like when her son's and her daughter's baby pictures floated off, and at what time and how her bed was no more. How many pieces did her yellow Louisiana-style raised cottage become? Where did each piece end up?

She takes the saucer with her cupcake and her silver cigarette pouch over to the sofa. Her Humane Society kitty Lucy buffs her ankle once Marie nestles in her place on the sofa, the dent in the cushion she has managed to create in six months. On the flat screen, the Weather Channel announcer stretches her arm toward a tropical depression that she energetically reports is near the Azores. Marie looks down at her saucer, which has a thin rim of silver paint. Where is the rest of her china? This trailer, this TV, this sofa, are no substitutes for her old things and for her old life. They drained Joe's 401K account to re-establish themselves here, since neither their insurance nor FEMA relief has brought them anywhere near being able to rebuild a $200,000 house like their old one.

What she has left is Joe, the saucer and a few poker chips. On top of that are the new unpaid bills and a suit against Nationwide Insurance, which recently sent them the premium renewal notice to insure the house that doesn't exist.

~ ~ ~

Until the last two hundred years no one—neither native American nor exploring European—kidded himself that nature and paradise were the same thing. The Caribbean peoples let Christopher Columbus in on hurricanes from the start. Haitian Caribs called their evil spirit Huracan, and urican was the name for a big wind on other islands. The Mayan storm god was Hunraken.

Maybe from the safety of Paris, Jean Jacques Rousseau could wax enthusiastic about the idylls of the noble savage. Gulf Coast explorer Pierre LeMoyne d'Iberville didn't share his optimism. D'Iberville had a French existential shrug for what he came across. (The English-speaking approach to colonialism leaned toward killing or at least chasing off locals who didn't cooperate with their arrival.) Interesting, but not paradise, was d'Iberville's verdict in his journal. Of a village north of the Bay of Biloxi, he wrote, "These Indians are the most beggarly I have yet seen, having no conveniences in their huts and engaging in no work." Harsher words went to earlier French explorers. De La Salle's priest's account of the area's geography and mileage was so wrong that d'Iberville pronounced the cleric "a liar that has disguised everything." A month later, he writes that he wished he had a Jesuit on board instead of the dimmer priests in his entourage. A Jesuit would be smart enough to figure out the language, he knew. D'Iberville was in poor health, but doesn't lament it in his journal. In the same spirit, he is cheerful and philosophical about how his crew fared in Biloxi Bay during his upland sortie. On his return, he "found all of my men enjoying good health except my petty officer, dead, and two sailors, one from disease and the other from drowning."

The idea of the idyllic seaside sprang from nineteenth century minds. Victorians ruled empires and expected their environment to fall in line too; across the world in colonial India, the British expected to have pianos hauled up mountains for their summer enjoyment. With that mindset, it wasn't hard for Mississippians to mistake the cyclical thirty-year hurricane lull for the fact that hurricanes had been eliminated, same as the Biloxi Indians.

The Tea Garden Hotel was one of the Six Sisters, the nickname for the half dozen resorts along the Mississippi Coast that drew New Orleans and Mobile visitors. They came to escape the yellow-fever season in town and to bathe in private wooden bathing boxes reached by stairs on the piers. Saltwater bathing was the rage for its health benefits. The Tea Garden Hotel held the record, with its pier for salt bathing stretching 800 yards into the Sound.

If d'Iberville had been around with his journal in 1860, he might have written that things were found to be fine on the Mississippi Gulf, except three hurricanes hit in one season and the Civil War was months away. The first 1860 storm prompted a New Orleans Daily Crescent report that however determined a woman might be, a hoop skirt was no match for a hurricane.

"Ladies who will wear hoops and will expose themselves to the vagaries of a high wind should be prepared for disaster ... We heard of several pitiable spectacles of ladies outraged by the wind on public streets." One month later, a stronger storm leveled all of the Six Sisters. When a Mobile-bound steamboat wouldn't change its plan and take them back to New Orleans immediately, angry survivors fired shots at the steamer. It departed in a hurry, leaving astounded refugees to camp on the beach for a week. A third hurricane came through on October 2, but the only thing left to damage was rubble from the other two storms.

If cornered, Coast natives admit hurricanes of a lifetime happen pretty much every twenty to thirty years, enough time for the percentage of storm veterans in the population to dwindle and for the community's memory to go soft. That was the case in Mississippi between 1860 until 1893. By then, railroads brought in northern snowbird tourists and dispatched seafood from the canning factories in Biloxi. It competed with Baltimore as the top seafood factory town in the country. Only a few days before the hurricane, downtown Biloxi received electricity—just in time to be knocked out.

~ ~ ~

The 1893 hurricane marked the first time a rescue effort was organized, not yet by the government, but by citizens. Battered boats returned with rescued survivors and reported more vessels and survivors marooned in the Louisiana marshes during the Sunday storm. Some survivors were found alongside bodies they were too weak to bury. At Tuesday midnight, two Biloxi seafood dealers dispatched the schooner Emma Hand to rescue more. It returned on Friday with gory stories, but no survivors. The death toll was listed as 1,848. In marshes, the skin had fallen off the dead. To come near, rescuers put camphor and whiskey on their nostrils and carbolic acid on the corpses. Some of the dead lived through the storm to die of exposure and starvation.

Although the U.S. Weather Service had been in operation for twenty-three years, the Coast received no storm warning. In the 1890s, the American Red Cross had a New Orleans office, whose sole achievement was to offer survivors clothing. Nine days after the storm, Biloxi's mayor organized a meeting at the opera house that produced a public drive to help families in the seafood industry. About a hundred large boats had been damaged. Several thousand dollars came in to the Biloxi drive from the New Orleans Citizens' Central Relief Committee. It noted along with the gift that "the question of state lines cuts no figure in this emergency." One year later, seafood production was back to pre-storm levels, and a railroad executive predicted, "There will not be a vacant lot where it is possible to build between New Orleans and Mobile."

A few years later, weather service warnings help mitigate damage from a 1901 hurricane. There was beach property destruction, but only one death, a visiting upstate cotton broker who shot himself in the head as the storm screamed.

In 1915, a storm arrived just as Confederate veterans gathered for an annual reunion. The Biloxi Herald gave top headlines to the convention, not the hurricane: "Biloxi is a Willing Captive of Confederates." Plans were for the veterans, then in their seventies, to march through downtown Biloxi. Instead, they took shelter at Beauvoir, Jefferson Davis's last home, while the live oaks crashed on Beauvoir's grounds. There was a repeat hurricane the next year, and at Fourth of July 1916, Confederate pensioners who lived at Beauvoir spent the post-storm day on the beach, collecting stray watermelons.

Once again, a thirty-year hurricane hiatus occurred. The jump from 1915 until 1947 was as mindboggling as the gap from 1860 until 1893. Instead of bearded old Confederates chasing down watermelons, the 1947 post-storm beach was strewn with slot machines and gambling tables, widespread but still illegal on the Coast at that point. At the Buena Vista Hotel, an in-progress Mississippi Highway Patrol convention hadn't evacuated. A day-after newspaper photo shows the fleet of debris-strewn ruined state patrol cars in the Buena Vista's parking lot. By 1947, Keesler Air Force Base and a roster of public agencies were around to take part in the response, including the Naval Reserve, the National Guard, the Salvation Army, the Coast Guard, the Merchant Marine and the Red Cross.

Then came category five Camille in 1969. With two-hundred-mile-per-hour gusts, its power was stunning. Its survivors were forever marked, yet not as fearers of hurricanes. They underwent a meteorological version of Stockholm syndrome. The community turned Camille's utter devastation into its top argument that hurricanes would be less trouble in the future. From one end of the Coast to the other, as surely as gravity, it was accepted as scientific fact that in Camille, the worst storm that could possibly hit had come and gone. The security of a property was measure on whether it survived Camille. In 2005, it became the cause of death of many of Mississippi's 231 casualties. Their strategy was to ride out the storm in places that withstood Camille. After Katrina passed that Monday, thousands of pre-Camille structure had been annihilated, including Beauvoir.

Memphis promotes its music, Washington the nation's heritage. U.S. seaside communities trade on their illusion as paradise. Sulfates and saturated fats raise consumers' antennae, but no one does much testing for toxins when it comes to a town's boosterism. A town's own residents may become the leading victims of the pitch for easy coastal living. A sermon always draws the most nods from the choir.

As a Biloxi newspaper reporter, I was happy to buy in. In my years on the Coast, I loved the fact that I didn't own a winter coat. I didn't need one: I did. The Coast is at Latitude 30 North, above San Antonio, Houston and Tallahassee. I can picture my blue, stiff hand opening the metal door to the newspaper plant one twenty-seven-degree day in January. More than I cared to face facts about my temperate North American town, I loved the idea of not owning a coat because I lived in a beachside paradise, or something like it. I happily deluded myself that I lived as a Gauguin girl in my white asbestos-shingle duplex, where if I craned my neck out the south window, I could see a speck of the Gulf.

~ ~ ~

No Coast baby boomer is a hurricane amateur. Marie and Joe were veterans of Betsy, Camille, Frederic and Ivan. Marie had been a teenager who taught swimming lessons at the Markham Hotel, made 32 on the ACT and surprised no one when she announced she was marrying Joe instead of going to college. Joe played guitar in The Mustangs, the best band on the Coast in the late 1960s. Joe was the one who opened every Mustang gig. When he belted, "Whoo, I feel good!" he sounded just like James Brown. Marie and Joe were the first couple to marry at First Presbyterian of Gulfport post-Camille. The sanctuary was repaired, but the air conditioning not running yet.

In 2005, Marie and Joe knew better than to stay home as Katrina approached. Their palm-flanked home was only two houses off the beach. They decided to ride the storm out at their daughter Stephanie's, fifteen miles north. Stephanie's house was at Diamondhead, a Hawaiian-themed 1970s subdivision above I-10. The subdivision had street names like Hilo and Molokai. The developers arrived too late to do anything about the name of the waterfront: Rotten Bayou. Settlers who prized plain words over illusion named it a couple of centuries before for the sulfur smell of the artesian spring that feeds the brackish bayou that connects with the Bay of St. Louis.

Looking back, Marie wonders why she spent the day before Katrina moving their eighteen-foot fishing boat inland instead of thinking to pack anything at the house. The boat was insured. Once they had the boat squared away, they headed to Stephanie's to spend Sunday night.

The family woke up Monday morning to screaming wind and rain. The wind had kicked in around four o'clock a.m. Water stood in the street at daylight. By nine, Rotten Bayou—like all the backwaters that fed into the Sound 15 miles south—rose along with the Gulf, part of the twenty-eight-foot tidal surge. Salt water seeped into Stephanie's house, and within thirty minutes, it was waist deep. Trees and house fragments floated by outside the sliding glass door.

The houses on the other side of Stephanie's street all stood four feet higher. Marie and Joe decided their group should evacuate and go to a neighbor's on the higher side. When Joe opened Stephanie's door, her big clay pots of red geraniums shot inside along with another two feet of water. The refrigerator fell forward. Joe's mother's curio cabinet, the sofa and television bobbed around the room.

They waded toward the street. In the driveway, the family's cars signaled distress. The burgundy Camry's trunk popped open, and its tail lights blinked in rhythm. The horn of the Tundra bleeped continuously, as did the red Celica's. As they crossed the street, they smelled the gasoline, which had formed a film over the flood water. Falling trees popped, interrupting the tenor wail of the wind.

They came in the neighbor's house through the garage. A pool table was in the garage, where the neighbor's mother, an Alzheimer's patient, was stretched out. As the wind screeched, she lay on the green felt unconcerned and corpse-still, only her white head sticking out from a blanket. Two Labrador retrievers paced around the table nervously.

Marie realized she was barefoot. Her shoes had come off in the current outside. The neighbors found her some tennis shoes and put a life jacket on her granddaughter Lindsey, who kept repeating, "My house is broken."

This house didn't stay dry much longer than Stephanie's. A few minutes later, water started creeping in. It followed the same pattern as at Stephanie's. It edged up to the top of the mother's pool table. The refrigerator fell over. The coffee table, lamps and chairs began circling the den. The neighbors decided to climb into their attic. They had an ax, in case they had to break through the roof. They rolled up their mother in her blanket, and the family heaved her mummy-like up the attic ladder.

Marie's family decided to evacuate again and found a way into an empty two-story house a few houses away. Joel, an employee and hurricane guest of Stephanie's neighbor, evacuated with them. Outside, they faced a shoulder-deep current. All the trees were down by this time. Broken trunks stuck out of the flood, and squirrels raced up and down them hysterically. Other displaced squirrels clattered over the exteriors of houses. As Marie and her family moved through the sludge, fuzzy brown spiders peppered the water. They stuck to Marie's shoulders and neck as she pushed toward the empty house.

In a few minutes, they made it to the vacant house. Even in the chaos, they felt uneasy about breaking in, as they stood at the lead-glass front door. Through the oval opening, they could see the first floor was flooded. The water, however, stopped six steps from the top of the stairwell. They could swim up the stairwell to the dry second floor.

Marie's son-in-law Anthony punched in the glass. The glass shattered, but the lead didn't budge. He worked his bloody hand through the lead framework and opened the door from the inside. Two of his knuckles were fractured, and glass fragments studded his hand.

One by one the group paddled up the stairwell. At the top, they crawled up to the safe second floor. They were dirty and barefoot once again. Their second round of shoes had come off between House Two and House Three. They found towels and wiped off the oily gunk.

Upstairs, there were bedrooms and a home office that had a door to the attic. This was the end of the line. There was no higher place they could go. The water continued to rise toward the top of the stairwell. For another thirty minutes, the water rose, from the sixth step to the fifth and on. It hit the top step. It was about eleven o'clock in the morning. The water stopped rising. They had made it. It began to recede. They hadn't eaten since the day before. Joel swam down the stairwell and found an apple for Lindsey in the refrigerator. In the kitchen cabinet, he found Pop Tarts and Vienna sausages. He later swam over to House Two and reported that his employer's family, including the mother with Alzheimer's, had survived in the attic. Meanwhile, Anthony waded back to his house and retrieved one of the five ice chests they had set up. Water still stood in the street, and he pulled back a chest of Cokes and beer. They dipped water from the yard to make the toilets work.

Marie never met the owner of the house where they survived the storm. She heard she was a recent widow, whose husband had been a lawyer. She understood the woman evacuated to Texas and never returned. The flood receded. Marie's group walked back outside.

At five o'clock p.m. Monday, the Diamondhead Fire Department transported the group to the Episcopal church in the subdivision. Its volunteers kept telling them the church was not set up to be a shelter. Marie's group walked to the Ramada Inn. It had neither food, water nor power, but it was crowded with refugees. There were rumors that the Red Cross would arrive momentarily with food and medical supplies. It never did. Meanwhile, a family renting two rooms offered one of theirs to Marie's group. Marie's family crowded on the beds and fell asleep Monday night without food, water or power.

Tuesday morning, Anthony walked back to his and Stephanie's home, which had flooded to the rooftop. He dug through the debris in his garage and found his bike. His Frito-Lay delivery truck was flooded and ruined, but his cargo had remained dry. He filled trash bags with Cheetos, Lay's chips, peanuts and Grandma's Big Oatmeal Cookies and peddled back to the Ramada Inn. He handed out sacksful of snacks.

Marie bummed a cigarette at the motel. It was her first in two years. Until then, she had made good on her vow to quit at Lindsey's birth. Marie got a ride to her brother's where she'd parked her green Toyota SUV. Her car was fine. Through the downed utility poles and five-foot high drifts of rubble, she and Joe navigated the SUV back to Long Beach. Eight blocks north of the beach, a policeman blocked the road. He looked at them blankly and shook his head. "If you live down there, it's gone," he said. "No one can get in. We're finding the bodies."

If you live down there, it's gone. She couldn't catch her breath. She gasped for air. She almost vomited. It was her first panic attack. She has had them regularly since. They begin when she starts to think about everything that's lost. It's as if she's replaying the same film in her mind. The movie goes from the image of one belonging to the next as she fights for breath and asks herself why she didn't pack her things, why she didn't appreciate what she had until it was gone.

It was twenty-four hours post Katrina. Marie was barefoot and in her same now-dry clothes. Home was gone. Joe needed his heart prescriptions. Anthony needed his hand treated. With a quarter tank of gas, they started driving. They headed north for a doctor and a motel room with electricity. Above the Coast lay the Piney Woods, an upstate Mississippi terrain of meager land and pine trees. County after county of timber acreage was flattened. Power was out for 150 miles. After a few hours, they found an open gas station with an hours-long waiting line. They decided the only way they would ever get gas was to fill a can. They bought two. Next open station, over the shouts of customers in line, they rushed up between gassing cars and broke in to fill their two cans. It was enough for Marie's Toyota to cruise in to Natchez on fumes.

They pulled into the Wal-Mart, still barefooted and in their dirty clothes. No barefoot customers, the Wal-Mart greeter announced. They argued. The greeter relented. They charged new clothes, shoes and a cell phone. Natchez had no empty rooms, but they heard some were available across the Mississippi River from Natchez at the Vidalia, Louisiana Comfort Suites.

Marie and Joe got a room, and Stephanie and Anthony stayed in the Comfort Suites' banquet room. The motel offered it to fifty refugees willing to sleep on the floor. On Wednesday morning, Anthony and Joe found the Natchez emergency room.

It was two days after the storm. They heard Coast homeowners now were being allowed back to their house site. Marie, however, couldn't bear to go. Joe and Anthony left her in Vidalia and went back to see the damage. In Long Beach, no house was left standing for blocks around. At 651 Trautman, everything was gone except the raised cottage's sixteen wooden pilings. Bundles of debris cluttered the yard. Their three-hundred-year-old live oak was still standing, dripping with gray rags and nylon fishing line.

No possessions were in the debris—no furniture, knick knacks, or clothes. Her Lenox saucer turned up in the neighbor's yard. Marie's casino I.D. appeared a few lots away. Joe took photos and brought them back to Vidalia. Every time Marie looked at the photos, she had a panic attack. They ended up staying at the Comfort Suites for fourteen nights, the charge for the last eleven picked up the by Red Cross, which eventually materialized.

Settling their insurance claim was next. It was a matter of returning to the Coast, finding a temporary place to stay, filing their claim and starting to think about rebuilding. They moved in with her sister Lou Ann, who lived five miles north of the water.

At this point, Marie's story is the same as thousands. It is the same as now-former U.S. Senator Trent Lott, once a congressional critic of junk lawsuits, who sued his insurer. Marie's homeowner's claim was denied. According to Nationwide Insurance, flooding destroyed their house, not wind. At first it seemed so impossible that she and Joe thought it was a mistake. Storm witnesses in three counties say hurricane winds lambasted Mississippi for four hours before the tidal surge hit at nine o'clock a.m. Eleven tornados were confirmed. Marie and Joe requested another adjustor. He said the same. They requested another and another. It was January when the fourth adjustor turned them down.

Marie and Joe's mortgage company had required them to take out a flood policy. That made them luckier than many who lost homes that had not been located in the federally set flood zones and had no flood policy. Their flood policy paid $137,000. It was a partial payment that excluded the roof and the windows. Contrary to the opinion of Nationwide, the flood adjustors blamed the roof and window destruction on wind. Marie thought the flood policy covered contents. It did not.

Their beachfront neighbor was suing Nationwide, and they hired his Florida attorney as well. At first, the lawyer predicted it would be a matter of a few months.

They just needed to hang in there, he said. Their trial was set for June 2007. They filed with FEMA for a $7,500 payment for Joe's lost car. When they checked back, FEMA reported it had lost their paperwork.

It was December. Her casino job was months away from returning. Her medical insurance had run out. Joe, formerly an industrial designer, was a disabled heart patient. They were now living on his Social Security check. The bills continued. Their mortgage company refused to accept the $137,000 flood-insurance check as settlement for their $200,000 house. It demanded they resume their mortgage payments. A collection agency has been writing that it may have no alternative but to repossess their house.

Marie's panic attacks continued. Her prescriptions cost $254 monthly. The doctor prescribed Xanax for the panic attacks and Zoloft for depression. She is a heavy smoker once again.

She dreads bedtime. She sleeps two hours at a time and dreams constantly that the storm is destroying her. She's escaping through water, but all that comes out of her mouth is "Ahhhh." She wakes herself up thrashing and kicking.

They couldn't pay off their mortgage, let alone buy another house. They couldn't stay at Lou Ann's forever. Joe heard about a trailer on sixteen acres ten miles north of the beach. It was in a tangle of eighteen trees that had crashed during the storm. The trailer had been repossessed. The previous owners hadn't relinquished it gently. They took everything they could manage—the kitchen appliances and the water pump in the yard—and while they were at it, they punched holes in the trailer ceilings. Field mice had moved in and scampered inside the walls.

Marie and Joe bought it with Joe's 401k and paid to clear the eighteen trees and refurbish the kitchen. They outfitted the living area with the blue and cream plaid sofa and the flat-screen television, on which they recently heard a news report that a man with the same last name as their Katrina comrade Joel, who swam for the Vienna sausages, had been pulled over for speeding. In the process, he was discovered to be wanted for murder in Houston for stabbing his alleged victim fifty-five times.

This is Marie's life these days. Her former supervisor called to offer her a dealer's job once the Hollywood Casino opened on August 31. Marie and Joe were glad. They needed the money, certainly. Just as importantly, Marie needed something to think about besides the hurricane and its consequence. Poker games have been her niche ever since casinos arrived on the Coast in 1992. In her dealer's chair, Marie almost feels back to normal. She can manage a smile wide and captivating as the Mississippi Sound itself.

~ ~ ~

Epilogue

Nationwide settled with Marie and Joe Cox for a fraction of their home-insurance policy amount. They remain on their sixteen acres inland—away from the Mississippi Sound—and have built a house behind the trailer. Marie still works in the Hollywood Casino poker room, although due to the economic slowdown, her hours have been cut back. Marie and Joe finally cleared their Trautman Avenue lot and put it up for sale. The BP explosion occurred a few weeks later. Since the oil spill, no prospective buyer has looked at their lot, where, as of the end of 2010, clean-up workers continue to clear tar balls off the sand. ▪

The Attributes of Water
Deborah Bauer

I REMEMBER HOW their house smelled. The fresh earth-toned paint and acres of carpet as untouched as just-mown grass. The house felt too new with the yards of swirling wallpaper still damp to the touch. They had the biggest house I'd ever seen, perched like a castle overlooking the airport and the San Francisco Bay. My cousin Mimi and her family had just moved in the week before.

In the pitch-black night, directly below my cousin's window, the empty swimming pool called, "Jump, jump, jump!" while across the room, my cousin drooled in her pretty dreamland. The images behind my closed eyelids rivaled those up on the screen downtown at the Fox Theater. I fretted over knives waiting in drawers, pills in medicine cabinets, even the Golden Gate Bridge that spanned ominously across the churning bay a mere sixteen miles away. I obsessed over all possible horrors in everyday life but I never would have done away with myself for real. I don't think.

At the window, I imagined my parents' mortification when they heard of my leap, with Mimi sobbing her big-baby tears as she told them that she'd been fast asleep unknowing of the tragedy until dawn. During the telling, a storm of grief would muddle her words while my parents asked, "Why, why, why?" trying their best to make sense out of a misfortune they'd never, for the rest of their days, fully comprehend. But finally they'd unite in a truce that couldn't have taken place without my demise. My mother's ruined chest would no longer matter because they had a more pressing crisis to deal with, the loss of their only child.

~ ~ ~

In the morning the soupy bay fog dutifully covered all traces of blue.

"It's working out so perfectly with you spending the weekend." Mimi tied a set of bikini strings at each jutting hipbone. She hadn't started to shave her legs and they shimmered with a blond, fuzzy down. "As soon as they start the hose we'll lay on the slope between the shallow and deep ends."

Lovely Mimi—all decked out in a new pink-checked French bikini—tied the strings at her stomach, then twisted the stiff cups around and up to her chest. A wedge of padding offered the newly sprouted breasts to the world, but it was plain to see that they were wasted on her. She played with them, dressed them up and admired them just like the Barbie dolls lined up on the shelf above her desk. They stood for the future: who she'd be someday. They had little to do with who she was now, a slightly stupid seventh grader.

Under my flannel nightgown, I pulled up a dull brown one-piece from last year. It barely stretched to my length. The cups were as empty as the year before. Mimi posed in front in of the dresser mirror with arms out-stretched, then brought her elbows together to make cleavage. After more than a minute of posing, she swam through the air in a slow crawl and talked at me through the glass.

"The water will cover us until we drown, or it will creep under and push us up until we float. The bet's still on, right?"

"Who gives a crap?"

I had more serious matters to stew over. My parents were on the Desert Dream Weekend at the Dune's Hotel in Las Vegas, Nevada, which included a room for two nights, buffet breakfasts and dinners, and two tickets to a show where women wore big feathered hats and little else. I'd studied the brochure which featured a bigger-than life genie in turban and pointed shoes, and a rooftop volcano that promised to spew an electric stream of lava every single minute of the day and night. The weekend was to be a celebration of the five-year mark since the sickness, and my mother was betting big-time with a suitcase packed with a sparkly cocktail dress, a sheer lavender peignoir set and a new black lace bra to hold her foam-rubber breast.

"Come on. You're stuck with me. You can do something my way, just this once, okay?" Mimi still whined like a baby.

"Oh, all right. But only one bet the entire weekend. I'll bet a dollar that the water will cover us and we'll drown before we float." I could have won a quick ten-spot if I was greedy. We'd done "Sink or Float," in sixth grade science two years before.

Mimi must have been daydreaming as usual. If an object weighed less than the water displaced, it floated. Eventually we'd float no matter what, but could we last with our faces covered until there was enough water?

"I say we'll float. It's a bet."

Mimi always took the side of hope, but then why not? Her life was perfection a-la-mode. She'd be gorgeous in a few short years with her long legs and white-blond hair. Her father was a doctor and they were swimming in money. But I was the most envious of her parent's lust for each other, a heat you could see like the shimmer above a highway in the desert, while my mother was in Vegas betting to win when even a thirteen-year-old could see that she'd already lost.

"You know what my parents will be up to as soon as the water heats up? They'll swim naked late at night when they think we're all asleep. They did it at our old house, too. I'll watch them from the window." She pointed to the one I had stood at the night before.

Most kids don't want to know about their parents' sex life—and can barely believe the facts of life when they see "Our Changing Bodies" in the sixth grade—but I believed Mimi. My parents had been old as dirt as long as I could remember. Even in pregnancy photographs, my mother resembled someone's fat grandmother in thick sturdy shoes and a bulging man's sweater buttoned all the way to her chin. All through elementary school, on the day of the school picnics my father stayed home while my mother perched on the edge of a green army blanket in girdle and stockings, watching the parents and teachers play softball.

She kept to the same routine day after day, completing housekeeping chores in the morning, then spending the long afternoons reading best sellers checked out from the library. When I walked through the front door after school, she rose to fix my after-school snack of four Oreos and a tall glass of chocolate milk. My father ate at six sharp then dozed in his special chair until bedtime. I couldn't remember the last time they had a conversation about anything besides an appliance needing repair.

Ever since the surgery, my mother slept alone in the master bedroom and my father on the lumpy sofa bed in the den. I think it started as a way to give my mother space in her recuperation, but even after her chest healed, he stayed away. Maybe they thought that I was unaware of the significance of their sleeping arrangement, but whenever Mimi slept over, my mother took over my room and made the same lame proclamation at bedtime. "I think it would be fun if you girls slept together in my big bed!" and Mimi always said, "Sure, Aunt Gertie!" amazed at the thoughtfulness, because in her world she'd never heard of an adult giving up a bed for a child.

In the kitchen we smeared raisin-studded bagels with globs of cream cheese.

"Let's get out there," Mimi said. She balanced her plate on top of a mug of orange juice, held her napkin under her chin, and with her free hand pulled the handle of the sliding glass door. "It's time to watch the workers. We don't want to miss our chance. I've already got big plans for my dollar."

Her father was on duty at the hospital and her mother had taken the twins to Little League practice. We were home alone. Mimi was ready to float but it'd be hours before we put ourselves to the test. We pulled our tee-shirts over our heads and flopped onto the chaise lounges even though the damp hovered above like a dreary awning. I shuddered.

Mimi reached over and poked my right cup with her forefinger. "You don't have much upstairs, do you?"

I plucked at my bathing suit until the dent filled in and resolved to stuff in a sock or two the next time. "Upstairs? That's exactly where I have it." I tapped my forehead three times.

"I'd rather have boobs than brains any day."

It figured. A bad idea to come for the weekend. Mimi had breasts that she didn't deserve. And mine, if they ever came in, would be probably be hacked off when I really needed them. I moved away to the far side of the yard, to one of the benches, spread my towel, and breathed deep of the new redwood. Four men dressed in white, from the covers on their shoes to the caps on their heads, smoothed plaster over the remaining patches of gray. The Beatles drifted from their transistor radio. "Yeah, yeah, yeah."

I wondered why swimming pools always looked blue when water was clear and plaster, white. A pool should look like water in a white bowl. I stood up on the bench and peered over the fence at the tiny San Francisco Airport. A plane lowered to the runway. Behind me, the workmen gathered their tools. The phone rang in the house.

Mimi rose and headed for the basement rumpus room. I stayed put but imagined a jackknife dive, a backwards flip, a somersault on the diving board hanging over the expanse of new, fresh, plaster. I watched the last few seconds of my life before my head burst open like a dropped bottle of catsup.

"Not too long now. Truce?" Mimi held a can of Coke in each hand and snack-size bags of Fritos tucked under each arm

"Truce. I'm just imagining this summer when we can swim everyday. I'm really looking forward to it."

"Let's eat at the beach." Mimi took the three new steps down to the pool floor. She spread her towel just behind the slope. She set out the drinks and chips for our little pool party. "It's going to be three, four hours, tops."

"You think so?" I spread my towel next to hers, edge to edge.

"Yeah. We have super water pressure here. My dad said so."

Water gushed from the garden hose and it seemed as though there should have been a wide silver nozzle under the diving board, something like a huge bathtub spigot. We slathered ourselves with a baby oil-vinegar mix.

"Yeah, my parents will do it on the stairs for sure." Mimi was at it again, as obsessed with sex as I was with death. "He'll sit on the top step. She'll sit on his lap, the slut. They're way too old. I just about puke thinking about it. Do my back." She held out the bottle and flipped over. I squeezed a blob of oil into my palm. Her skin felt hot and thick, like an animal's hide without the fur.

"So don't think about it. And you mean straddle. She'll straddle his lap." I set down the bottle and stretched out.

"Yeah, Brain-Drain. Straddle like a horse. Giddy-up. Maybe I'll go wake up the little guys. They're old enough to know what's going on with those two perverts. Don't worry. They won't be scarred for life. I'll make sure to wake you up for it too if you're lucky enough to be over." She smiled her sick little smile.

"No thanks. I don't know why I listen to you." I longed to drive home, to get in a car and turn the key, take off and never feel trapped again, but it'd be three long years before I had that kind of freedom. I was sick of always being thrown together with Mimi just because we were related. Everyone thought that we were real friends. What bullshit.

Mimi rolled over to bake the other side. "Do my front." She giggled.

"Do your own front."

Hour after hour we went baked and burned until our backs and shoulders took on the pink of the stuff in the bottle. Eventually we emptied the pool of cans, trash, and even the towels. The only sounds were the occasional chirp of a bird, a muted honk, the faraway drone of a plane. Then all of a sudden a ball hit the fence followed by a scuffle at the gate. The twins were back. Joel and Danny burst into the yard. Their mother, my Aunt Shelly, followed in her summer uniform of shorts and a halter-top knotted at the back of the neck.

"Well, looky here at the bathing beauties at the beach. Rachel darling, we want you over here every day in the summer. Get your parents over, too. How's the water? Must be chilly." Shelly grinned her big-toothy smile. Her yellow-blond hair was the color of lemon peel. It was impossible to believe that this woman and my mother came from the same union.

"God, Mother. Go away. Please." Mimi closed her eyes and turned her head, willing them off to some faraway cornfield. Shelly's flip-flops slapped the deck as she circled the yard checking the coping, the plaster, and the tile.

I pretended to sleep until I dreamed for real. I woke with ice water nipping at my heels and Mimi staring into my eyes. "I've had enough," I said, bored beyond human endurance.

"Well, I'm staying put. I said I'd stay until I floated and I will. I don't give up."

I scooted back and watched the water, chilly as melted snow, seep under her butt. How long would she be able to stand it? I started to feel guilty for knowing the outcome, for being the smart one, for always having the facts. "Come on, Mimi. Let's go in and get something to eat. We missed lunch and I'm starved."

"Not on your life. You just want to win."

Her brothers slammed through the gate again and dropped their bikes on the new decking. Joel yelled from across the pool. "Mom, how come Mimi gets to go in there already?"

The sliding glass door opened and Aunt Shelly came out wiping her hands on a dishtowel. "Go back in the house and leave the girls alone. Put your bikes in the garage please. You're not bringing them into the backyard ever again, and don't forget it." She shooed the boys back through the gate and followed close behind.

Inches of water rose up the side of Mimi's torso, but still, her bottom met plaster. The bet was off as far as I could tell. I stood. "Come on, cousin. You don't have to pay me. Let's go into the house. I've had it. We've wasted an entire day."

"No way."

"What do you mean, 'no way'?"

"I'm not leaving until I float. I don't care how long it takes. I don't care if you're in or out. You're a chicken. You always give up too easy. I'm staying put until the end."

"What if the water covers your face and you can't breathe?"

"I have it all planned out. You'll hand me a straw. Go get them. Ask my mother."

"I don't think so. We never talked about straws."

She gave a quick shiver as the water crept across her flat stomach. Her breasts rose like two round pink islands. The water covered her ears and threatened her freckly nose. God, she was an idiot.

"Come on Mimi. Give it up. You aren't floating and won't be in this lifetime. I'm going to let you in on a little secret, the scientific theory on floating. You have to have more water under you than displaced by your body. Comprende?" I tried to simplify the concept for her inferior mind. "In other words, you'll drown before you float for sure." There. The surface of the water looked cracked in the sun.

"I don't believe you. You're always so full of crap. Go get the damn straws."

In the kitchen, Aunt Shelly pulled cups and glasses from the top rack of the dishwasher.

"Do you have any straws?" I didn't say why I needed them and she didn't ask. My mother would have wanted to know why on earth I needed straws when she didn't see a glass of liquid in my hand.

"I know there are some around her. I'll just have to find them." She dug through drawers and cupboards filled with every conceivable paper product and finally located the thin red and blue box buried under wax paper, napkins, and foil. She handed over the box. "How's the pool filling?"

"Fine."

"I'll bet your parents are having the time of their lives. Tomorrow night we'll get to hear all about it. I can't wait. We haven't been to Las Vegas in years. They're going to see the fancy ladies with the feathers and ... so exciting!"

And glittery breasts, I thought. Two on each dancer. They would never allow a woman with one. The world was simply not made for left-handed people or one-breasted women. How would my mother feel when she finally figured it out, when she came to terms with reality? The trip was a bad idea all around.

Shelly leaned back against the counter and giggled with a glass in each hand as if she knew one of those nasty adult secrets, but she knew nothing outside of her cozy little life, her swimming pool sex, and her happy, healthy trio of kids. My Aunt Shelly was incapable of understanding that two days and nights in a Las Vegas hotel room was not enough to fix a marriage, that my mother's ruined chest would be a map of scars forever charting her course. And what about me? I'd been wondering if my mother was going to die ever since I could remember, wondering if cancer was lurking in my own skin, organs, and bones.

I held up the box to remind her that I had things to do, places to go. "Well, got to get a move on," I said.

I found Mimi at the bottom of the pool pinching her nose with her thumb and forefinger. Maybe she sat up and cheated while I was gone, but maybe not. She wasn't smart enough, but by now I really didn't care. We could name her the victor, the winner of the day. She could have my dollar, two dollars in fact, but I knew she'd never give up so I got in beside her. She grabbed the box, took two straws and handed the box back before she reclined into the water. I wondered what it felt like to be so submerged and sure about things. I put two straws in my mouth and tossed the box on the deck. My lips formed a makeshift seal. I thought about letting the straws slip away, letting the water rush in. The end was there for the taking. No muss, no fuss. It would be so easy to let the water run down my throat until I was dead. No waiting to turn the steering wheel into the oncoming traffic, no diving out of Mimi's nighttime window. Splat. My parents united in their grief.

A mounting pressure pounded between my eyes. It was quiet, not completely, but like the echo when I put my ear to a seashell. I relaxed my feet, my stomach, neck, and found that I wished for Mimi's innocence. Part of me believed if I could hold out long enough, anything was possible.

But then I felt it, heard it too, a gigantic splash, the crash of matter breaking the water's calm surface, the muffled shrieks, the hooting of little boys, and the dim calling of my name, "Rachel, Rachel, Rachel." A basketball bobbed next to my head. I sat up and there was my mother, a full day early, kneeling on the curved cement edge, in her nylon stockings, looking into the pool.

"Come on Rachel, get out and get dressed quickly. Your father is waiting out in the car." Her features were shadowed from the late afternoon sun; was her smile real?

"Did you have a good time, Mom?"

"Everyone has a good time in Las Vegas."

Mimi stood, hunched and shivering. "Rachel, did you see me? I floated! It was so cool, so very, very, cool. You owe me a dollar."

I had to believe them. Both of them. What else could I do?

BOOK REVIEWS

Citrus County
By John Brandon
McSweeney's Rectangulars, 2010
224 pages
$22.00

Reviewed by Jolene Barto

John Brandon's novel *Citrus County* asks questions. One pervasive question kept tickling the back of my mind as I read it: "What exactly *is* this book?" Crime novel? A coming of age piece? Postmodern thoughts on American culture, on adolescence, on American American-ness? A book Dostoevsky-esque in its quest to pose questions about morality and human conscience? The answers to all these questions, to the main question, is simply, *Yes.* Yes, it's that. And that. And *that.* And a lot more.

Citrus County, in all its many layers, is essentially the story of three trouble-makers stuck in a tiny section of Floridian landscape. Something is already stewing inside Toby, a boy barely old enough for his voice to change. In his mind, a bunker—one he has found on his many hikes in the sandy Florida forests—is inextricably linked to him and his evil destiny. It's here that Toby expects to hear the words that will confirm that he is destined for higher evil.

Then comes along Shelby Register, a foreigner from Citrus County. She's smart as a whip and not afraid of what people, especially Tony, think of her in the middle school they both attend. Toby and Shelby are inevitably drawn together. It's a meeting of the minds, but one initially initiated by Shelby, who relentlessly pursues Toby, forcing him against walls for kisses.

Mr. Hibma, the school's geography teacher, completes the trio of subversive characters. Mr. Hibma views himself as a "character in a novel" instead of as a teacher in Citrus County. His fantasies of killing the school's very appropriate English teacher, Mrs. Connor, give him his only respite from "kissass" children (as he calls them) and the condominium lifestyle. The murder scenarios he concocts in his head keep him afloat. Her murder is his only purpose.

Brandon could easily have written a quiet novel about a trio of misfits who happened to be occupying each other's spaces. Instead, he lets something go terribly, terribly wrong. Suddenly, Shelby's baby sister, Kaley is stuffed into Toby's duffel bag. Toby has listened to the bunker and it has demanded sacrifice. Here, in the bunker, Toby keeps the kidnapped Kaley hostage. By doing so, Toby changes the landscape of his own, Shelby's, and Mr. Hibma's lives.

And the book is never the same after this.

The subject of kidnapping is rendered with grace and subtlety. There are no gruesome descriptions of Kaley's situation or of the days that stand on end in the bunker. There is only the subtle horror of Toby's actions, of Shelby's reactions, of the town's response in general to their new circumstances. The FBI agents coming into town are simply movers of the prose, not major characters. And there's never a question of whether Toby will be caught. He will not be—Brandon is explicit about that. The tension is tangible without being stereotypically terse. *Citrus County* is not formula crime novel, and it never feels that way.

Brandon continually keeps his characters searching. Not that there are any answers, necessarily. In the last part of the book, Toby finds another abandoned space, one in which he can listen for the truth again. In a warehouse store's garden section, he discovers a hose and trails it to its spigot, pulling himself toward the wall. He turns on the water and soon feels the hose stiffen in his hand. "Every plant in every row, the rotting and the unruly," Brandon tells us, "was due a share."

And perhaps that is the novel's greatest accomplishment: its ability to subvert the details, to skirt around the elephant in the room. There is something unassuming about Brandon's writing. No fingers are ever pointed. No one completely becomes the victim. All the characters in *Citrus County* are both empathetic and horrific. Their flaws are not glazed over, but neither are their goodnesses. They are characters with grit, characters that you are never sure you can trust, but want to all the same.

The Particular Sadness of Lemon Cake
By Aimee Bender
Doubleday, 2010
304 pages
$25.95

Reviewed by Shannon Hall

Aimee Bender's *The Particular Sadness of Lemon Cake* throws its readers into a world of magical realism where food reveals emotions. Its plot is definitely unique. On her ninth birthday, when Rose Edelstein sneaks into the kitchen to eat a piece of the lemon cake that her mother has made from scratch, she discovers that she can taste the emotions of people through the food they prepare. At nine years old, Rose is literally forced to swallow the secrets and fears adults carry quietly on their shoulders.

A simple ham sandwich is not so simple to Rose. "Good ham, flat mustard from a functional factory. Ordinary bread. Tired lettuce-pickers. But in the sandwich as a whole, I tasted a kind of yelling, almost. Like the sandwich itself was yelling at me, yelling love me, love me, really loud." Rose can identify everything from the town the factory food is made in to the farmers who select the ingredients. She sees food in complicated layers and is forced to deal with each layer as she chews, and usually forces, her food down. The tired lettuce pickers can be determined and so can the girl who made the sandwich for an inattentive boyfriend. Rose feels the emotions of every person who has made any ingredient in the food and sometimes resorts to Oreos and other junk food because they offer less human contact.

Rose becomes infected, as do Bender's readers, with the burden of others and their deep feelings, their complicated problems. While she sits alone in the kitchen with her mother's stolen cake, Rose finds herself "tasting a distance" she somehow knows is connected with her mother, "tasting a crowded sense of her thinking, a spiral, like I could almost even taste the grit in her jaw that had created the headache that meant she had to take as many aspirins as were necessary... ." She tastes her mother's guilt and later discovers her affair. This is quite a weight for nine-year-old Rose to carry through the novel. It forces her to grow up faster, and it affects the relationship she has with her father.

Mystery arises when it turns out that Rose's brother, with whom she seems to have little relationship, due mostly to age difference and sibling rivalry, also has a secret. Her lonely brother, her unsuspecting father, and her sneaky mother keep the story interesting, and her brother's secret will keep you guessing until the last couple of pages. But the novel is about something deeper. As you follow Rose from elementary to high school you watch her struggle with loving someone fully, faults and all. Furthermore, Bender laces the novel with comic relief. Just when you think the story is getting too tense, you will find yourself laughing out loud.

Rose keeps her gift a secret from most of the characters in the book. She knows that her gift is not normal. She is aware that if people believed her, they would think she was strange. The few people she does share it with need convincing. She has to eat the food they prepare and then describe the emotions she tastes to win their faith. Rose's character is very convincing. She is nine, and as a reader, I too felt like I was nine years old. I was back to the time of wishing for summer vacation and dreading homework, fighting with siblings. Bender's novel reminded me of times when things were supposed to be simple. I felt like a kid again as I spent my weekend turning page after page.

Breaking into the Backcountry
By Steve Edwards
University of Nebraska Press, 2010
192 pages
$16.95 (paper)

Reviewed by Carrie Gaffney

In 2001, Steve Edwards, a writer and teacher at Purdue University, won the PEN/Northwest Margery Davis Boyden Wilderness Writing Residency. His prize? A five thousand dollar stipend and seven months alone in a cabin on the ninety-two-acre Dutch Henry Homestead in Oregon. *Breaking into the Backcountry*, the memoir resulting from this experience, is a layered examination of solitude, nature, and, ultimately, gratitude. "The wilderness is where people get lost and die," Edwards writes. "The wilderness is where people go to find themselves." Part travel writing, part nature writing, part meditation, Edwards' memoir takes readers deep into the backcountry, as well as deep into what it means to be alone in a culture such as ours.

The narrative begins as Edwards makes his way from Indiana to Oregon, newly divorced and wary about the realities of his upcoming seven-month situation. With the closest town two miles away, no electricity, and no running water, Edwards has a lot to learn about both running a homestead and, of course, about running it alone. As Edwards and his father make their way into the backcountry, they decide to take their time and visit some of the parks along the west coast. In a poignant moment, Edwards realizes that they have come to a park to admire its storied redwoods, yet he does not know how to identify one. It is the first many such encounters he will have as he adjusts to, and then begins to thrive in, the solitude of the place.

Although he does have an occasional human resource, including Bradley Boyden, one of the homestead's owners, and a few invited and uninvited guests, the closest regular companions Edwards encounters during his time at Henry are the bears and deer that roam the area outside his cabin and the mice that keep him awake at night. In the absence of any human adversaries, the mice become his greatest source of frustration. Ultimately, these mice become a symbol not only of Edwards' initial loneliness and his anger with himself, but also of his eventual acceptance of his own flawed existence.

As the novelty of his new situation begins to wear off, Edwards becomes accustomed to mornings of writing, afternoons of outdoor work, and restless nights, all the while wrestling to find the balance between solitude and isolation, between regret and peace. During his seven months alone, Edwards experiences the death of his grandmother, memories of his separation from his ex-wife, and the events of September 11, 2001; throughout these events, he uses the space the solitude creates to find new meanings and deeper insights. And as he heads back home to Indiana, he makes a commitment to retain that space as he re-enters his old life.

Even on the surface, Edwards faces a daunting task as a writer in that he must capture a life foreign to virtually every potential reader: a life of few distractions and of even fewer characters. Unlike Thoreau's two-year experiment in solitude, which Edwards invokes several times in the memoir, his own experiment includes no cabin to be built, or friends less than a mile away. Still, the life of a homesteader is arduous work. Thus, much of the narrative serves as an illustration of the daily struggles he encounters, both physically and emotionally: fishing, gardening, animals, compensating for loneliness.

Take, for instance, these words as Edwards attempts to describe his experience as a part of the sunset on the homestead:

> The cloud is so big and cleaves so closely to the mountain that everything around me—the long grass in the meadow, the red-dirt driveway, my own skin—also turns pink, glows. I look at my arms, at my hands.
>
> I am an ember.
>
> But as much as this sudden becoming thrills me, it is followed a moment later by melancholy, because I have no one to share it with. And I start to wonder: How many visions just as mighty and beautiful have I already seen and forgotten since coming here? How many epiphanies will no one else ever know, or that even I might not remember? Then, something strange. I hear a voice inside my head, but it's not my voice.

Along with Edwards' description of his new life on the homestead comes a deeper narrative that speaks to his new understandings about the natural world and about who he is, which he does without sounding preachy or self-indulgent. During these moments, Edwards is at his best, and his training as a poet emerges.

Breaking into the Backcountry is much more than a fish-out-of-water story.

It serves as fine example of the impact memoir has on multiple audiences. Fans of nature writing will appreciate Edwards' eye for natural detail; fans of travel writing will enjoy reading about Edwards' mishaps as he makes

adjustments to his new geography and learns the ropes of a life outside
of Indian; fans of lyrical writing will come to love how Edwards is able to
appreciate the sacred within his daily life.

Embryos & Idiots
By Larissa Szporluk
Tupelo Press, 2007
71 pages
$16.49 (paper)

Reviewed by Chet Weise

Larissa Szporluk 's *Embryo and Idiots* shimmers with originality. It follows a
near science-fiction narrative arc, with the world at its beginning made from,
and literally populated by, rock. Like the best science fiction, *Embryos and
Idiots* presents a narrative about humanity, but from a unique—aka alien—
viewpoint, through the central character of Anoton.

To further aid the earthbound reader, Szporluk introduces all three
sections of her book with a quote from Milton's *Paradise Lost*. These short
introductions clarify the intent of each section by drawing parallels to
Milton's story of the fall of Lucifer from Heaven. In addition, other references
ground the poem in familiar Biblical mythology. Szporluk's use of simple,
clear diction and parsed lines also helps to stabilize the ambitious book for
readers.

The poem-story begins in a land made of mineral and metal where
plant life and other biological life are outlawed. The first stanza of the first
poem, "Boulders," establishes that the main character Anoton's mother is
in violation of that law: "He knew she was hiding a bee. He could hear it
/ zapping inside her, trapped in the amber / nook that led to her mineral
uterus." Hence, conflict about relationships, sexuality, emotion and control
immediately arises. This passage demonstrates something else important to
satisfying the reader: musicality. Szporluk uses the subtle chiming of assonance
(the "e" sounds) and alliteration (the "r" sounds) along with slant rhyme
("ZAPPing" and "trAPPed") liberally throughout the book. Rhythmically,
the lines have roughly the same pattern of 2-4 stresses. The caesuras are also
consistent. The uniform rhythm and diction within each section buttresses the
wilder science fiction imagery (i.e. "mineral uterus") and plot.

The third person speaker also introduces the growing conflict within
Anoton's own soul regarding its emotional condition. Consider the poem's

last stanza in which Anton watches his mother's bee: "of which he had been enamored, /like a pilot of a bomb site, fingering the lever." His conflicted attachment can be seen in the simile of the bombardier and is furthered in the next line: "...This century wants anything. Is that a soul?" But the same society that "wants anything" assassinates a mother for possessing a living creature. The book's exploration of the paradox of control versus passion within society and within Anoton's person drives its plot and arc. In "Idol," Anoton finally betrays his mother to the king, his father, who "had her crushed" and the bee killed. In society's eyes, Anoton did right, but interestingly, the bee haunts his conscience:

> But no matter how
> hard Anoton shook,
> the bee was a silent
> guest ... a defiant sponge
> that shriveled up in spite
> of what supplied it.

Here are the first hard moments highlighting the struggle between soul and soullessness or emotion and the emotionless. Compounding the emotional confusion, in "Reaper" Anoton's father avenges his wife's death despite his own laws. He beheads Anoton. The head, large and made of rock, plummets like Milton's Lucifer to the world below. And like Milton's Lucifer, Anoton turns from the fallen into something like a ruler: his head turns into an island, a life-spring. More personally, he becomes attached to a new character, a nameless woman implicitly associated with his mother. She delights in watching Anoton grow emotionally—for now he who essentially assassinated his mother for harboring life now makes it. The irony and paradox are unmistakable.

In the second section, the island of Anoton is growing. Poems become stichic, with more direct rhyme. Lines are shorter. The point of view varies from first to third person and voice shifts among Anoton, Society, Nature, and the Woman. With more life in the poem, more emotion follows, resulting in a less cohesive narrative. There's the feeling of change.

In the final section, Anoton becomes fully emotional; consequently, the newly populated biological world created from him awakes with his emotionality. And, Anoton never finds forgiveness or love from these others—life is pain. For clarity, Szporluk parallels the climax to Biblical archetypes like Adam and Eve, Lucifer's fall, and Noah's Ark. Accordingly, the book ends with "Satan at Length." The mythological snake waits "last in line behind the cattle" to board the Ark. The poem's last lines define his role, "as the plunger the plumber pumps / to unclog our kingdom / of memory's crud / I come in handy, without meaning." The snake Satan realizes his practical worth. And thus the book ends, as Szporluk intended, with a "yawn."

Nashville Chrome
By Rick Bass
Houghton Mifflin Harcourt, 2010
272 pages
$24.00

Reviewed by Jonathan Ashley

While the film *Crazy Heart* garnered several rave reviews as well as some Oscar nods, bringing attention to the novel of the same title on which it was based, many quieter voices commented on the film's lack of originality and substance. The novel, likewise, received as many pans as it did praises. The story of an alcoholic has-been country crooner trying to facilitate a comeback is nothing new. From *Tender Mercies* to *Walk the Line*, the story's been done more times than that of the reformed thief.

With *Nashville Chrome*, author Rick Bass delivers both style and substance; it's the story of the Browns, three siblings who make it huge in Nashville between the era of the Carter Family and the era of Elvis (a young Presley is actually a supporting character, endearingly drawn and full of manners and wonderment). Jim Ed, with his bass voice and stellar guitar ability, is quiet and reserved most of the time, but hell on wheels when depressed or celebrating. Bonnie is gorgeous but tom boyish, true to her country roots. And Maxine is the prima donna, the most talented of the three, but also the most selfish and destructive.

It is Bass's obvious familiarity with country life, with the detriments of fame and ambition, and with the importance and difficulties of having a tightly knit family, that separates his novel from more pedestrian fictional music bios. Critics and academics first took notice of Bass upon the publication of *The Watch*, a collection of short stories that seems to make it on the favorite list of every modern popular literary fiction author. And it is the terse, honest yet poetic prose that made Bass's short fiction both cerebral and utterly readable that will win the hearts and minds of most people who pick up *Nashville Chrome*.

None of the chapters spans more than five pages, and while the novel could be labeled, "episodic," a clear plot arch sustains the story. Bass takes us back and forth chronologically between the Browns' rise to fame and fall from grace and the obscurity and isolation of the modern day Maxine Brown, the once-accolade-hungry star of the group, who now lives in the hills outside of Nashville, forgotten for the most part by modern country music fans. While billboard stardom passed the other two siblings by, their humility allowed them to continue to find happiness in life. The reader does not know until the final pages whether or not Maxine will come to terms with her guilt, ambition and loneliness or if she will make a comeback. And while those questions make for interesting devices to help propel the plot forward and develop characters, the real question is whether or not the Brown family will ever be as close as they once were, when they were children singing in the Alabama wilderness to forget their father's raging alcoholism, trying to maintain their wonder and innocence.

Much as in Stephen King's *The Body* or Dennis Lehane's *Mystic River*, what makes the reader feel such tenderness and affection for the characters stems from the novel's genesis, from the by turns joyous and tragic memories of the Brown's adolescence steeped in poverty and desperation. Even when Maxine reaches the pinnacle of stardom, she is still not satisfied. It is fitting that she is the member of the trio who finds herself dealing with alcoholism, for, as anyone familiar with addictive personalities will attest, it is not stardom itself that she seeks, but rather something to fill the void in her created by tragedy, neglect, poverty and abuse.

This is something new to the form; neither in *Crazy Heart* nor *Tender Mercies* is it ever explained why country singers are such psychological train wrecks. *Nashville Chrome* not only gives logical reasons as to why Maxine, Jim Ed and Bonnie are broken, but it also shows how they all deal with their broken family history differently.

Jim Ed can't stay still for too long. He's addicted to the road and to gigging.

Maxine, despite overcoming alcohol, still allows the broken home she was born in to rule her life by isolating and dreaming of a come back filled with standing ovations, applause and even a biopic.

But it is Bonnie, the bedrock of the group, the spiritual guru who kept them from plummeting even sooner, who goes to tremendous spiritual and mental lengths to grow from the pain of her past.

And in the end, it is Bonnie who is responsible for the fate of the Browns.

The real tragedy does not lie in the history or future of the Browns. It lies in the fact that this novel did not come out earlier, in which case the film rights would already have been bought, perhaps preventing its comparison with subpar works like *Crazy Heart*.

Strangers in America
by Erika Meyers
Bottom Dog Press, 2010.
134 pages
$16.00 (paper)

Reviewed by Christopher J. Lessick

In his "General Prologue," Geoffrey Chaucer chronicled a cross-section of pilgrims en route to Canterbury in Medieval England. Similarly, Erica Meyers presents a cross-section of the contemporary working class in Cleveland, Ohio in her first novel, *Strangers in America*. While there is no literal pilgrimage, the narrator goes on a figurative pilgrimage, visiting homes and businesses as an exterminator. Winner of The Great Lakes Novel Prize, *Strangers in America* truthfully chronicles the present moment of financial difficulty for working class America.

The novel follows twenty-eight-year-old narrator Helena Adamzik, an exterminator-in-training who rides with different coworkers to learn the intricacies and etiquette involved in destroying pests and rodents. Self-righteous enough to have left journalism because her editor continuously slanted her articles, Helena is only sort of like the sympathetic college grad who takes any job she can in order to pay the perpetually overdue rent. However, she deftly inserts that information long after the reader has come to love Helena. Meyers hatches an ingenious framework to tell a story that combines humor with timely and timeless themes of paranoia, relationships, survival, and (un-) employment.

Helena is first found "standing in a stranger's bathtub, fully clothed," remembering her new boss's only advice, "When you leave the room nothing should be moving." She piles up visions of customers, including a businessman rubbing her ass "like he was expecting a genie to come out of it." Meyers laces this strong narrative hook with irony, as Helena is anything but promiscuous or victimized in any way. Instead, she seems cut of that upper Midwest, blue-collar fabric, with a strong work ethic and a desire to continue to learn and improve at her job, however unappealing that job may be.

Conflict resonates from all fronts—in the form of a landlord who threatens eviction, a mother who dislikes Helena's job, and her ex-boyfriend who fights over money. It often arises with the unexpected characters, too—psychiatrists, gun-hoarders, addicts. "You need to hear about the impact of the cruelty you expose these animals to on a daily basis," a woman who has let Helena's groundhog go free accosts Helena when she goes to check a groundhog trap on a Saturday. In another scene, a guy with the right side of his face "stitched up like a football" asks, "Are you going to kill it or stare at it all day?" In yet another, Helena endures a long drive with her ex-boyfriend so he can sell his prescription pain medication to pay his overdue share of rent.

An exterminator shows up and takes care of a problem, often in one visit. Likewise, the reader gets glimpses, and is able to enter the stories of Helena's clients at his/her own risk after peering inside the doors she's opened. In one example, a man extinguishes his cigarette in the top of a human skull on his desk and prepares to write a check. Most of the clients and their stories are believable, and readers will understand and appreciate the sincerity of Meyers' portrayal of this cross-section of society.

Perhaps the only downfall of *Strangers in America* comes from the reliance on dialogue tags for enhancement, which comes off as mundane or unrefined at times. Instead of the traditional "said," Meyers tends to overwrite, using, "repeat," "warns," "confirms," often adding "as..." phrases to (over-) animate the characters while they speak. Yet at other times she goes on for a page without a single dialogue tag. This seems excusable for a young writer; certainly a consistent style will emerge in her future work.

Strangers in America is a cathartic ride along the road of middle class America. Erika Meyers has crafted a story, rich in humor and irony, in which the events, characters, and situations are likely to ring true with readers from all walks of life. Meyers grew up in working class neighborhoods in Ohio, and it's likely people haven't changed much from those she observed while riding with her exterminator father as a young girl. As her title suggests, even those in the same class are strangers to each other, especially in this moment of financial uncertainty where people must do what they can to survive—sell prescription drugs, break into and sleep in other people's houses, or take jobs for which they are educationally overqualified.

Sag Harbor
By Colson Whitehead
Doubleday, 2009
273 pages
$24.95

Reviewed by Barbara A. Lee

Colson Whitehead has stated that it was his intent in *Sag Harbor* to give readers a glimpse into black culture that is not usually highlighted in literature. This coming of age story takes place not only in a specific time in recent history (the 1980s), but also at a significant psychological time in the main character Benji's life (adolescence).

Benji's family dynamics suspiciously resemble the Cosby Show, the number-one-rated television show in the 1980s. Benji's father is a doctor, and his mother is a corporate lawyer. Benji attends private school and makes the rounds of Bar Mitzvahs. Due to his polite manner and grasp of the English language, he is mistaken for the son of a diplomat. Because Benji leads a somewhat exotic hybrid life where money meets race, the average African American may have some difficulty connecting with him.

The story is told through the adolescent lens of self-absorption. Every summer. Benji unmasks and journeys to Sag Harbor, where he becomes one of a gang of young African American males. Whitehead could be making a commentary on the social mask that professional African Americans wear out of necessity. Like Benji, the further we move from the eyes of the dominant culture, the more relaxed we become. However, reality hits home when a white couple enjoying a walk on the beach recoil from the black youth. Their unfounded fear of him and his friends is the first of many experiences that spotlight the shift from innocence to experience.

Benji and his younger brother Reggie live in the family summer home during the week, and their parents come down on the weekends. Out from under the parental watchful eyes, the brothers shed their civilized skin. The reader gets a glimpse of the adolescent male world—social hierarchy, Darwinism at its most basic level—with the added texture of race. Benji constantly tries to figure out his position in the pecking order. He is lower on the social ladder in the wider society, but within the black community he is near the top rung.

Whitehead uses Benji for close up shots and the decade of the '80s—in which both Benji and African American culture experience growing pains—for the wide-angle shots. (If the Civil Rights Movement was the birth of modern black culture, then the '80s were its coming of age.)The freewheeling '80s, framed by Doug E. Fresh and Rap Music's age of innocence, blockbuster movies, and the Pepsi vs. Coke beverage wars, are as primal as Benji. On a societal level the reader is treated to a culture fixated on brand names. Benji's brother Reggie insists on wearing Filas. "I thought I didn't want you buying these cheap paper plates anymore," Benji's father says. "Look at this. Why didn't you listen to me? What do you think I am? You treat me like I'm some kind of goddamned pussy."This is a close up shot of the fragility of the black male ego. Benji's father is a doctor, who insists upon being respected in all things. At the height of his profession, he can be decimated by his wife's insistence on cheap paper plates.

As an adult African American male, Benji won't be able to unmask as easily as he does for summers in Sag Harbor. Going from boy to man, he will lose the freedom and innocence of childhood. Like his father before him, he will wear the mask as he straddles the fence in an attempt to maintain a balance between his race and economic status. The beauty of *Sag Harbor* lies in its ability to offer a different perspective of black life while simultaneously exposing the hidden psychological specters that haunt a people uncomfortable in the light and the dark.

The Good Soldiers
By David Finkel
Picador, 2009
316 pages
$ 15.00 (paper)

Reviewed by Megan Scholl Lindberg

The Good Soldiers is a must read for anyone who wants to hear the stories the media wasn't broadcasting during the surge that began in Iraq in January 2007. David Finkel, the journalist who follows the men through their fifteen month deployment, takes the reader to the battlefield, to the forward operating bases, the hospitals and into the homes that the soldiers left behind. He speaks too of Iraqi customs, of Iraqi lives. In this war, the enemy doesn't stand on the front line but rather in a home, an empty building, or in a neighbor's yard, and ignites an explosion that rips limps, breaks open backs, and slices heads, feet, and hands. Humvees are engulfed in flames and the survivors struggle with images of their fellow soldiers' brutal deaths, while they hunt through innocent or maybe not so innocent Iraqi homes for the man, woman or child who pulled the trigger.

When the soldiers of the 2-16 infantry plan their burial services before their deployment, they do so nonchalantly, the same way they attend briefings on stress management and suicide prevention. It finally falls to a chaplain to shock them out of their nonchalance. "This is important," he says. "If you are not ready to die, you need to get there."'

The U.S. Army's Lieutenant Colonel Ralph Kauzlarich led the eight hundred soldiers from Fort Riley, Kansas into Baghdad with his favorite phrase "It's all good." The battalion's average age was nineteen. This was the age of Duncan Crookston, whom Kauzlarich would later see at the U.S.

Army Institute of Surgical Research Burn Center lying in a hospital bed with his wife and mother by his side, having overcome the loss of his ears, nose, eyelids, legs, arms. Kauzlarich presented Duncan with a Combat Infantry Medal and the Army Commendation Medal. Duncan nodded, that nod a spark of hope, of triumph.

Still, when it came to one of his best soldiers being sent home for Combat Stress, Kauzlarich's views were conflicted. He could see Duncan's injuries, but he couldn't see Adam Schumann's. "Losing a leg couldn't be faked...But to lose a mind?" The surge, though, was Schumann's third deployment. In his mind's eye, he kept seeing "his first kill disappearing into a mud puddle" and "a house that had just been obliterated by gunfire, a gate slowly opening, and a wide-eyed little girl about the age of his daughter peering out." Adam had reached his breaking point, and now he waited for the Red Cross helicopter to come for him. As the battalion's physician assistant said, "'There's not a physical scar, but look at the man's heart, and his head, and there are scars galore.'"

For most of Ralph Kauzlarich's deployment, his wife sent him loving emails, and enjoyed the sound of her husband's voice being played from the memory chip inserted into their young children's stuffed animals. But the stress of being a single mother took its toll, and, frustrated, she wrote to her husband: "I stayed up two extra hours last night to get all the details straight... I've been making all the decisions here for ten months by myself..." Finkel writes the sacrifices, the occasional joy, the heartache and the frustrations of all involved.

Finkel doesn't try to tell one story. He tells many. He even tells that of an interpreter who stands by the Americans as she lies to her fellow countrymen in order to protect herself: "I am from Syria." The interpreter than turns to the soldiers and says: "I'm not bad like my people."

The Good Soldiers forces us as readers, too soon after a soldier's death, back into a mission, when our minds are still tender. We are there for the heart-racing anxiety of approaching a trash pile in the street or deciding which road to take back to base, all the while anticipating the tick, click, boom of an explosion. It is pure chance that saves some—a bullet barely grazes one soldier's lip, and the third humvee gets hit instead of the first. As the wife of a good soldier of the Iraq War, I can say that this book is the closest I've come to understanding the fears and emotions that trap my husband in a state of mind that I can't always reach. It is a book to read and keep in our homes—tuck it away for future generations.

The Haunted House
by Marisa Crawford
Switchback Books, 2008
71 pages
$14.00 (paper)

Reviewed by Gretchen M. Oberle

Marisa Crawford's first book of poetry casts open the door to *The Haunted House*, giving us a provocative tour of form and function—dense prose poems interspersed with free verse poems—through which we become the walls, the closets, the very house. Here we find a place to live and breathe in memory along with the past inhabitants of this house. Crawford's speaker twists with urgency, meditative perspective and pop culture references. Her substantial prose poems appear on the page with the weight of age and time; they beckon us to focus on minute detail of the past, to slide into fluffy slippers, baggy t-shirts and banana clips, to pine over fashion, love, and friendship. Her free verse recalls the haste of flighty youth, tapping out the syncopated rhythms in anaphora.

If we listen we can hear the voices of this house speak as they pull image after visceral image out into the light for our examination. The title poem moves us through the life of the speaker as if communication can only be given or received through a series of image flashes, yet the language whispers in our ear like the phantom of a teen girl with a hard crush on the neighbor boy. A girl who knows more than we suspect...

> 17.
> When you press her button, Barbie says, *Math class is tough!* Press it
> again and she says,
>
> *I think it's something too complicated to*
> *be simplified in a way that makes it possible to explain it in terms*
> *of how what I want is probably rooted in ideologies that are fueled*
> *by capitalism and therefore somehow violent and reactionary and*
> *Somewhat problematic in some respects.* Press it again and she says,
> *Let's plan our dream wedding!*

There is an acidic tang to some of these poems, reminiscent of the bites Anne Sexton would remorselessly take from reader, speaker and poem.

Crawford weaves a sense of the confessional throughout her poetry. We know the poems are written in retrospect so there is a certain filter of age, but we should not be fooled by that, as Crawford succeeds in transplanting us through time and space to teach us what it is to see the world through the eyes of a teenage girl. But not just a teenage girl, rather a girl who is growing, who is processing, storing and integrating her life experience on every possible level.

Not only do we find a confessional speaker here but we find the seeds of a feminist view, as she addresses the blatant 'dumbing' down of girls by use of toys ("*Math class is tough!*"), by use of fashion ("*Let's plan our wedding!*"). She holds a finger pointed to the signs of guilt and manipulation that hold a girl, a woman, in a single space. In the poem "Tidal," we are asked "If beauty is a dead girl / a garden / would you lift up her skirt?"

The Haunted House is a collection of poems for the senses, memory, teen angst, love and the incessant flow of change. It brings us to a place that we rarely visit as we age, a place where our perceptions have transformed and color our past in wholly different hues; we stay, we listen and watch as memory races forward in vibrant color to remind us where we came from, whether we shared our life with the girl in this haunted house or one on our own street. If we are patient, if we absorb what the house reveals we will find deeply significant truths between layers where "There was a red-hot lava river flowing down / the fissure between bed and wall, / hard to see through all of the steam."

A Mountain of Crumbs
By Elena Gorokhova
Simon and Schuster, 2009
305 pages
$26.00

Reviewed by Nora Hall Burton

Imagine that you live in a country where you must stand in line for hours for the most basic necessities: milk, bread or flour, and that before you reach the head of the line, the milk you waited for is gone, and there is no more. Imagine also, that in this country your children sit at the table, hungry, waiting for you to bring home the milk, crying for food you cannot give them. Perhaps you might invent a game to help your children ignore the hunger that burns in their bellies. You might crumble a piece of black bread and a sugar cube into piles to trick your children into thinking they have more on their plates than they really do. This is exactly what Elena Gorokhova's grandmother does in *A Mountain of Crumbs*, a memoir of growing up in Leningrad (now St. Petersburg) during the 1960s and 1970s. The mountain of crumbs becomes a metaphor for life in the Soviet Union.

The fear of the Stalin years was replaced by isolation in The Soviet Union, first under the leadership of Khrushchev and later Brezhnev in what became the "era of stagnation." Life behind the "iron curtain" during the cold war was repressive. The State took more control of the arts; the economy was slowly eroding and the political outlook distrustful. In this environment, Elena Gorokhova grew to young adulthood, curious, intelligent and skeptical about communism. "The rules are simple: they lie to us, we know they are lying, but they keep lying anyway and we keep pretending to believe them." Her mother was a professor of anatomy and her father ran a trade school. Of her mother Gorokhova writes, "Born three years before Russia turned into the motherland, my mother became a mirror image of my motherland: overbearing, protective, and difficult to leave. Our house was the seat of the *politboro*, my mother its permanent chairman." Elena is often at odds with her mother as she is with the State. In spite of the fact that she is overbearing Elena loves her mother very much. "There must have been a time," she writes, "when my mother was cheerful and ironic, before she turned into a law-abiding citizen so much in need of order." The family was by Soviet standards middle class: apartment dwellers who knew that theirs was not a life of abundance but a life of just enough.

Elena Gorokhova writes with unflinching honesty and a bit of wry humor of the human cost of life behind the "iron curtain." Totalitarianism was the order of the day, ordinary and expected. In third grade, Gorokhova dons a red kerchief and joins the Young Pioneers whose motto is "always ready." She recounts the story of Pavlik Morozov, a Pioneer hero of the past. Pavlik, the son of wealthy peasants, told the authorities that his father was hiding sacks of wheat in the basement when people were starving. The boy was given a medal and the father sent away to the camps in Siberia. "We all know that some things are so obvious you just don't debate them. You don't debate what's written in history textbooks. You pretend that you think that Pavlik Morozov was a true hero deserving a medal, just as in nursery school we pretended to chew the bread with rancid butter."

The human cost becomes evident when Gorokhova's father is admitted to the hospital after many months of wasting away at home. Her mother makes her call the hospital, at age ten, to get a progress report on her father, and she is told by a woman with an unemotional voice, "Died last night." As Gorokhova notes, "We hear a lot about love for the motherland and love for the Communist party, but never about love for one another."

Gorokhova begins her study of English in third grade. She soon learns she loves the language and becomes a willing and apt student. Gorokhova discovers the English word privacy for which there is no Russian equivalent. Gorokhova currently lives in New Jersey with her husband of twenty eight years. Her mother and sister live in America also. As the mother of an American daughter her life has changed as has her motherland. "My daughter's native language is English and KGB and Pravda are just the names of expensive bars in New York," she writes. A *Mountain of Crumbs* is not only interesting to read but also difficult to put down. Gorokhova's love of English is evident on every page as she writes with honesty, integrity and heart.

Contributors' Notes

Jennifer Atkinson is the author of three books of poems—*The Dogwood Tree, The Drowned City*, and most recently *Drift Ice*. Her poems have appeared recently or are forthcoming from *Field, Image, Witness, Cincinnati Review, New American Writing*, and others. She teaches in the MFA program at George Mason University in Virginia.

Deborah Bauer has contributed to *The Salt River Review, Poetry Midwest, Quiddity, Crab Creek Review, Boston Literary Magazine*, and the Jewish feminist journal *Bridges*. She earned an MFA from Antioch University, Los Angeles.

Mario Chard is the poetry editor for *Sycamore Review*. His poems have appeared in *Indiana Review, RATTLE, Poet Lore, Sugar House Review, Georgetown Review, Western Humanities Review*, and elsewhere. He currently teaches creative writing at Purdue University.

Jeff Fearnside lived and worked in Central Asia for four years. His literary writing about the region has appeared in several publications in the U.S., including *Rock & Sling, Etude: New Voices in Literary Nonfiction*, the anthology *A Life Inspired: Tales of Peace Corps Service, Permafrost, Rosebud Magazine, Potomac Review, Crab Orchard Review*, and *Bayou Magazine*.

Ellen Ann Fentress has written on Hurricane Katrina for *The New York Times* Modern Love column, and has also contributed to *Oxford American* and *Southern Women's Review*. Her last *Oxford American* essay "Intimate Strangers" was selected as a recent essay of note by the *Wilson Quarterly*. In 2009, she won the nonfiction Emerging Writer prize from the Southern Women Writers Conference. An MFA graduate of Bennington College, the Mississippi Delta native writes on Southern culture and politics as a journalist. She teaches creative nonfiction at Millsaps College in Jackson.

Ruth Goring is the author of the poetry collection *Yellow Doors*, published by WordFarm in 2004. Her poems have appeared or are forthcoming in *Comstock Review, CALYX, Raving Dove, RHINO, Alligator Juniper, Chicago Quarterly Review, Pilgrimage*, and elsewhere. She works as a book editor for the University of Chicago Press.

Scott Gould has contributed to *The Kenyon Review, Blood Orange Review, Carolina Quarterly, Black Warrior Review, Yemassee, New Stories from the South*, and *New Southern Harmonies*, among others. He lives in Greenville, South Carolina where he teaches creative writing at the South Carolina Governor's School for the Arts and Humanities.

Karen Holmberg is a poet and creative nonfiction writer whose work has appeared or is forthcoming in such magazines as *Quarterly West, Southern Poetry Review, West Branch, Cave Wall, Potomac Review, Black Warrior Review, New Madrid, Poetry East*, and *Cimarron Review*. She teaches in the MFA program at Oregon State University.

Randall Horton is the author of *The Definition of Place* and *The Lingua Franca of Ninth Street*, both from Main Street Rag. He is the co-editor of *Fingernails Across the Chalkboard: Poetry and Prose on HIV/AIDS from the Black Diaspora*, published by Third World Press, 2007. He earned an MFA in poetry from Chicago State University and a PhD in English/creative writing from SUNY Albany. He is an assistant professor of English at the University of New Haven.

Teresa Milbrodt has contributed to *Nimrod, North American Review, Crazyhorse, Cream City Review, Hayden's Ferry Review, CutBank*, and *Sycamore Review*, among others. Her short story collection *Bearded Women: Stories* will be published by ChiZine Publications in Fall 2011. She earned an MFA in Creative Writing from Bowling Green State University, and is a professor of creative writing at Western State College.

Peter F. Murphy grew up in Alexandria Bay, New York, the Heart of the Thousand Islands. He is the author of *Studs, Tools, and the Family Jewels: Metaphors Men Live By*, and served as editor for the collections *Fictions of Masculinity* and *Feminism and Masculinities*. His essays and reviews can be found in *The Review of Contemporary Fiction, Twentieth Century Literature, Modern Fiction Studies, College Literature, Signs*, and *Feminist Studies*. Murphy's first published poem appeared recently in *Birmingham Poetry Review*.

Matthew Nienow is the author of two chapbooks: *The Smallest Working Pieces* published Toadlily Press in 2009, and *Two Sides of the Same Thing* published by Southeast Missouri State University Press, 2007. His newer work has appeared in *Best New Poets, Indiana Review, New England Review, Prairie Schooner*, and *Willow Springs*. He has received awards from the National Endowment for the Arts, the Bread Loaf Writers' Conference, the Dorothy Sargent Rosenberg Memorial Foundation. He's also the recipient of and two Individual Artist Grants from Seattle's leading arts organization, 4Culture. He holds an MFA from the University of Washington and is currently attending the Northwest School of Wooden Boatbuilding in preparation for opening his own boat shop.

Anthony Opal lives in Chicago, Illinois, where he is a graduate student at Northwestern University. His work is forthcoming in *Harpur Palate, Boston Review, Redivider*, and *Notre Dame Review*.

Kristian Ansand Walter contributed the photographs for Jeff Fearnside's nonfiction piece "Ships in the Desert." He was born in Dresden, in the German state of Saxony, and now lives and works as an editor, photographer, and videographer in Leipzig.

Nikki Zielinski is a Cleveland native and a University of Oregon MFA candidate. She is the grateful recipient of Northwest Review and SLS Fellowships, a Centrum New Works Residency, and the Miriam McFall Starlin Poetry Award. Having lived in nearly twenty cities, she finds it difficult to stay put, and distracts herself by running, studying medieval Italian swordsmanship, and reading aloud to her dog, Bruce. As usual.

Reviewers

Jonathan Ashley is a Louisville-based book dealer whose short fiction has appeared in *A Twist of Noir, Yellow Mama*, and *Crime Factory*. His novella "They Can Kill You but They Can't Eat You" is being tuned into an independent film.

Jolene Barto lives in a haunted house in Murfreesboro, Tennessee. She works as waitress and student, and is finishing a novel.

Nora Hall Burton is originally from Detroit and now lives in the central Kentucky area. She is completing a memoir.

Carrie Gaffney teaches writing and reading in Indianapolis, where she is also an active teacher-consultant for the Hoosier Writing Project. Her work has appeared in *Kentucky Monthly Magazine* and *School Talk*, an NCTE publication.

Shannon Hall tutors school-age children and writes freelance articles for local newspapers and hospitals.

Barbara A. Lee is a creative artist and a licensed professional clinical counselor in Paducah, Kentucky.

Christopher J. Lessick teaches British and world literature at Great Bridge High School in Chesapeake, Virginia. He lives in Virginia Beach.

Megan Scholl Lindberg is a Chicago native and a creative nonfiction writer who works as a legal assistant at a large law firm. In her free time, she travels and works on her memoir.

Gretchen Oberle teaches at the Purdue extension in Richmond, Indiana. In addition to writing poetry, she maintains an art studio in her home working with various types of media.

Chet Weise is a poet and musician. Most recently, his writing has appeared in *We Never Learn: The Gunk Punk Undergut, 1988-2001*, an anthology of stories about the U.S. punk scene, and *Pine Magazine*.

Artist's Statement
Western Waters
Sant Khalsa

Western Waters addresses the commodification of nature, water as consumer product, and human desire—a never-ending thirst.

I am fascinated by the necessity and absurdity of these stores, and the way these venues have come to represent the source of a natural experience. Of course, these stores are merely elements of entrepreneurial enterprise—constructed sites to provide the consumer with the most essential requirement for life and survival.

The success of these stores is based on consumers' fear that their tap water is not safe to drink and on providing an alternative to bottled water. Today, plastic bottles have replaced earthen vessels, and to fetch our water, we travel in polluting automobiles to and from this fabricated representation of a river, well, or spring.

I have photographed nearly two hundred locations in California, Arizona, Nevada, and New Mexico. These images will serve in the future as a historical document, either registering a fleeting fad or laying the foundation of what will become commonplace in our society.

~ ~ ~

All photographs from the *Western Waters* series are 6 x 7 inch gelatin silver prints. You can view more images from the series online at santkhalsa.com.

Sant Khalsa, *Cool Water, Los Angeles, California, 2002*

Sant Khalsa, *Good Water, Montebello, California, 2002*

Sant Khalsa, *Crystal Fresh, Pomona, California 2002*

Sant Khalsa, *Water to Go, Covina, California, 2001*

About the Artist
Sant Khalsa

Sant Khalsa (b. Sheila Roth January 3, 1953, New York, New York) is an artist, educator and activist living in Southern California since 1975. Her artworks develop from her inquiry into the nature of place and the complex environmental and societal issues present and visible in the landscape of the American West. Her works have been shown in more than 100 solo and group exhibitions internationally, and have been acquired by permanent museum collections including the Los Angeles County Museum of Art, Center for Creative Photography in Tucson, Nevada Museum of Art, UCR/ California Museum of Photography, and others, in addition to private and corporate collections in the U.S. and Europe.

Khalsa is a recipient of prestigious fellowships, awards and grants from the National Endowment for the Arts, the California Arts Council, the California Council for the Humanities, Arts Foundation of San Bernardino County, the Center for Photographic Art in Carmel, and others. Her artworks are widely published in books including Art in Action: Nature, Creativity and Our Collective Future (Natural World Museum and Earth Aware Editions 2007), The Altered Landscape (University of Nevada Press 1999), Fotofest H2O 04: Celebrating Water (Fotofest 2004), and Post-Landscape: Between Nature and Culture (Pomona College Museum of Art 2001) and other publications including WaterWorks: Contemporary Quarterly (No. 4, Summer 2006), Connecticut Review (Fall 2005, Vol. XXVII, No. 2), and European Photography (No. 75, Summer 2004). Articles and critical reviews regarding her artwork can be found in Art in America, Art Ltd., Afterimage, Exposure, British Journal of Photography, LA Weekly, New Art Examiner, Coagula Art Journal, ArtScene, The Los Angeles Times, Artweek, Visions Art Quarterly, PDN/Photo District News, The Boston Globe, and High Performance.

Khalsa has presented more than fifty lectures at professional conferences, art venues, and universities including The Getty Center, Los Angeles County Museum of Art, Society for Photographic Education, Western Historical Society, American Photography Institute at New York University, Art Center College of Design in Pasadena, Claremont Graduate University, and California Institute of the Arts (CalArts) in Valencia.

Khalsa was cited in the *Forbes Collector* (September 2006, Vol. 4, No 8) feature article "Hidden Gems of Photography" by Weston Naef, Curator of Photographs at the Getty Museum, as an artist worthy of collector's attention in the current photo market, and also by art curator and critic Kim Beil in the January 2007 Art Ltd. article "Powers of Ten" as one of ten contemporary Los Angeles photographers who are " . . . earning their place in history and giving compelling shape to the future."

She is Chair of the Art Department and a Professor of Art at California State University, San Bernardino where she is one of the founding faculty of the Water Resources Institute (WRI).

POETRY

INTERNATIONAL

An annual journal of poetry & translation
from around the world

John Ashbery
Jorge Luis Borges   Li-Young Lee
Kamau Brathwaite   Philip Levine   Adrienne Rich
Toi Derricotte   Ewa Lipska   Marge Piercy
Carolyn Forché   Osip Mandelstam   Luis Omar Salinas
Marilyn Hacker   Dunya Mikhail   Charles Simic
Seamus Heaney   Valzynha Mort   Gerald Stern
                          Ý Nhi   Gary Soto
                                                 Marina Tsvetaeva
                                                 Derek Walcott
                                                 Amir Saadi Youssef

visit us online
www.poetryinternational.sdsu.edu

Send 3-5 poems of your best work to:
Department of English and Comparative Literature
San Diego State University
5500 Campanile Dr.
San Diego, CA 92182-1040